Billy Lee
my name —
Bill Lee (Goddard)
Sounds
more Korean!

"Ture Nongak"

Korean Common-labor Farmers Music and Dance
An historical novel

Enjoy!

by Billy Lee

xulon PRESS

Ture Nongak
Korean Traditional Common-labor Farmers Bands
by Billy Lee

Printed in the United States of America

ISBN 9781619046580

www.xulonpress.com

ACKNOWLEDGEMENTS

This work is in memory of beloved In Bok/Mercy Grace, an inspirational Korean educator and child of God. Deep thanks to the courageous generation of committed and devoted-to-God Koreans of the south who have withstood the rigors and the threats, activated by the enemy of our soul.

Thanks to my beloved parents and to those friends who endured through the trials of writing.

Great appreciation to Dr. Douglas Feaver, the prime motivator for this work. Much gratitude for many others, including associates in Youth With A Mission, William Carey Int'l. University, beloved at The Church On The Way, Gordon Patten and Nancy D., and my home-church brothers and sisters for selfless editing, and more.

Last, and most importantly, I thank and dedicate this to the eternal, ever-merciful Father who has given me more than a billion brothers and sisters—and a whole world— with whom to share great joy and abundant life. Thank You, YHWH.

Preface

The nation now called Korea has one of the richest histories of any country. It is hoped that this work will enable the reader to be better informed about that rich background—to be enriched, and to be better able to do intercessory prayer and to see that wonderful peninsula unified for God's glory!

There is a section of militarily-dense land in Asia. It has the highest concentration of battle-ready troops in the world. On either side of this potential powder keg spread the two, now-separate parts of a once unified nation. To the north is the super-Goliath, a new strongman, who has been 'developing' in size and strength for more than fifty years, against reason and tradition! About sixty-five years before that growth happened, accumulated centuries of natural development fed and nourished that place. It had been under attack from without; relatively, a spiritually-dark place.

This is the Korean peninsula. The time is ripe for victorious *Battles of Righteousness*. The North of the Korean peninsula is that 'God-defying giant'.

The call is to pray and to intercede for Korea. The light will soon overcome the darkness through Almighty

God's supernatural response. Thus, freedom for an oppressed people of more than six decades will follow. There are vitally important, national Korean issues, which are obscured by the enemy of our souls.

In this age of 'cyber sin', global terrorism, and the potential for instantaneous, genocidal holocausts, spiritual battles will rage unto a mighty victory, for Christ— who has won the victory! Now is the time for salvation, and issues of great spiritual importance are to be brought before the throne of God. It is our responsibility as sons and daughters of God to claim the plunder, by engaging the enemy for the salvation of souls! Claim the victory!

Creative people, all made in God's image, are called to arm themselves for battle (Eph. 6:11-18). God's purpose is always that gifts He has given will glorify Him. Often, those gifts have been stolen and corrupted by Satan, to be used for worldly pursuits. The gift of indigenous, traditional, Korean music and dance was given to the Korean peninsula long ago, subject to the one who came to (kill,) steal (and destroy).

Being immensely forgiven, forgiveness must undergird our hearts toward all, including the government and people of Communist, North Korea.

This is a call to a righteous, cultural-revolution, that Christ would be glorified, and acknowledged as Creator, Savior and Lord. The cultural gifts that God has given to Korea must be reclaimed by His people. The grace of God and His love will be the means that the people will accomplish the awesome task. Therefore, it is an objective of this work to inspire to prayer and action so that peace, reconciliation, and the salvation of God would prevail throughout the Korean peninsula. May the hand of *Hananim* facilitate that.

The true history of Korea is the basis of the call to write this historical novel. Redemptive values in the culture and social sphere should be given serious consideration. A form of collective farming practiced in Korea resembles the 'kibbutzim' of Israel. *Yet, this form of socio-economic lifestyle can truly succeed ONLY in a Christian/Judeo-Christian context.*

References to selected Korean words presented as footnotes are used to 'share the vision'.

CONTENTS

CHAPTER I

THE OLD AND THE NEW

"FARMING IS THE DIVINE GIFT AND GREAT WORK BASIS OF THE WORLD" the large banner reads, emblazoned in the Korean language. The son of a South Korean farmer lofts the banner high upon a single, vertical pole, as he sticks it in the ground, and

1

the shadows cast by the hills which surround, protect and enclose this small village have drawn near. His father stands amidst the abundant hills, beautifully and wonderfully scattered and twisted-about, put in place by the Intelligent Designer, from the beginning of time, in this 'Land of Morning Calm' [1]. The hills contribute greatly to the unmatched beauty and identity of Korea. Like his father, the son cherishes everything involved in the unique farming lifestyle, which he is inheriting from his father.

'Farming is a millennia-long treasure for Koreans' is the thought which fills the mind of the elder-farmer, his heartfelt response to the banner's message. He watches as his farmer-son carefully re-positions the banner's pole for maximum visibility on the rice-paddy's bank at the foot of the large hill, the village's namesake. The white banner displays its message radiantly, in the cool, morning breeze, as the rice-paddy smell fills the valley and hills. Within the village there is unanimity of agreement with the banner's message. In other parts of Korea, some would strongly disagree

Young Kim is just entering his twenties, and he is a combatant. His battle ground is the world of farming, *and* music. Yet, his weapons are not those visible in military skirmishes. Like his, other 'combatant-units' are being trained in co-operative farming villages. The training is simply to live the farm life and to play music *in the context of God's love!* Both Young Kim and his father, Kyung Jae, fight the normal, traditional farm battle against the seemingly capricious impulses of natural cre-

---

1. *Chosun*,

2

ation. They both also battle another enemy, a "master" of unseen forces, which stands against them.

The warming air invigorates the sturdy father as he surveys the panorama of rice fields. Because he feels touched by this rich land's long, deep history, the father silently reflects. 'Tradition in Korean farming has adequate parallels to the economically acclaimed, agricultural practices in Israel of the cooperative *'kibbutzim'.'* He further muses that, in *that* fact may be found an ally. Many Koreans hold to the traditional, rural Korean, motto that farming is a divine gift—as do these two men.

Although this idea is *traditional,* still, such an ethos of *non status quo* thinking equips Young Kim with a sense of belonging, and a strong sense of awe.

Young Kim is the lead singer of the redeemed V*olunteer-labor Association, Farmers Music and Dance Band*[2]. The band calls Suwon-san home here in a farming village central South Korea. Kyung Jae's assignment has been to evaluate and delegate responsibilities needed for the advancement of the agricultural community. That task has revealed many special gifts of the members of Suwon-san. He helps prepare the way, so that those diverse qualities will be discovered, developed and exercised. He sees, not only the abilities of his own gifted son, but the abilities of each village member—abilities given and used, to bless one and all. He is convinced that they are to be held with all gratitude, esteem and profound respect. Therefore, the diligent farmer believes they should be fully utilized.

---

2. *Ture/Doorae nongak.*

As the leader of the village *collective-labor association*, [3] Kyung Jae looks up with some reverence, at the banner. The banner not only broadly proclaims the cultural values of the village, but also speaks as a literal and symbolic sign of freedom in discipline and faith. It stands to reflect and to permanently establish their sincerely-held beliefs of hard-earned and time-earned values. This man has experienced the blessing of God's grace-innumerable times. Times of prayer and obedience to God were and are frequently rewarded by very rich harvests and at other times by the avoidance, of 'normal, natural calamities' which commonly afflict other villages, nearby!

The cost of certain other types of 'calamities' is dear, including centuries of invasions and oppression-from-without and internal national fractures, which would include the most recent fraterno-genocidal, politically generated war, whose deep scar still remains in the hearts of the Korean nation.

"The lifestyle of the redeemed collective-labor association is a committed lifestyle, Young Kim," his father says, punctuating his own time of self-reflection that he had.

"And, without our God—the God of our ancient ancestors—whom they called, and we call *Hananim*, [4] we can do nothing. Commitment is based on the principles upon which this lifestyle is established, the same prin-

---

3. *Ture/Doorae*
4. The primitive and contemporary Korean name of the Highest Deity/God of heaven.

ciples that allow it to continue. Korean, *Farmers music*[5] was given birth by the Common-labor Association's needs and abilities," he concludes.

The inherited farm model for these men is millennia-long, the once-popular, traditional manner of the local Korean, farm-based, Common-labor Association. Integrated with that, is the musical band; a necessary and essential combination. "Always remember this *Common-labor, Volunteer-labor,* or *Collective Farmers music* [6] is the unique and special gift to this land, Young Kim," his father says to him, firmly but gently. "Your valuable role in the Farmers band is proof that the 'others-focused' lifestyle has generated 'cultural, musical offspring' that the entire village loves."

Unable to conceal the excitement of 'something new' that had reached the area, Young Kim answers, "Yes, father, and almost the whole country knows about *Specialized* farmers music. It is different, *'The Specialized farmers bands'* are professionals who tour throughout the country, father," Young Kim says with resonant excitement in his voice.

"Young Kim," his father sighs and begins to explain, "the knowledge of some of the richest parts of our rural history has been lost to all but a few. Do you remember that Common-labor Farmers music and dance had, at one time, virtually completely disappeared from this land? Many factors have contributed to the music genre's near disappearance. This music was established as a vital part of the farmers' life, and of our ethnic heritage," his

---

5. *Nongak—nong is farm/farmers, ak is music (and dance, in this context).*

6. *Ture/Doorae Nongak*

father says. "Even the Chinese have said *for centuries* that Korea is 'the land of the people who sing'. Chinese visitors would always hear, all throughout the day, the joyful sound of our ancestors singing while they worked in the fields. Our rural ancestors would sing all day—just as you still do!

"Commitment is its own reward for this lifestyle, Young Kim," his father continues to instruct his son. "The longer time that you commit to this life, the more you will see each village member increase in worth." Kyung Jae's son knows that his father speaks with the certainty of much experience. But, something is distracting the young man from being able to grasp the importance and significance of his father's words. To complete his thought, Kyung Jae begins again, "Most of our countrymen and women are very familiar with Specialized farmers music, but most know or remember very little about the diverse paths of the background heritage of that lifestyle. Nor do they know about Common, or Volunteer-labor Farmers music. Few know the latter is the prototype lifestyle, which, now, so much later, everyone here practices and lives.

"This village shares a priceless gift, Young Kim," his father continues. "This gift, when held in the perspective of faith, can produce unity, happiness, co-operation, and efficiency. In addition, we discover efficiency in our health, finances and relationships. Like so many other Korean *Volunteer-labor farmers* [7], your mother and I, and so many others here in the village are often scarcely able to believe that great gift! We are scarcely able to believe that typical, daily, hard and repetitive farm work

---

7. *Ture/Doorae nong.*

\

could become something joyful—and someth
would love to do each and every day of our l
Young Kim is a true gift!" his father says, hap

Kyung Jae briefly reflects, and hopes to snare with his son as the family priest. So he says, "Soon, we must leave to do what has been planned for us, today, Young Kim. But, let me say something, first. I see that you have learned that your responsive singing in the field serves to unite us in our hearts. At those times, all who sing are brought close to one another. Even though you are separated and at a distance in the field from the others while you play, there is real closeness. We know that remarkable closeness is inherent in responsive singing. Also, we both know that there is a spiritual element that fulfills the already achieved closeness.

"Please listen closely, son. You and I have learned this from ancient history. I would like you to know this and pass it on to your children as I have, to you. These historical facts have actually impacted the history of this country, and a great part of the world.

Kyung Jae smiles again, and begins to speak, "We know that an ancient Chinese Emperor-king decreed that he, and only he—in all of China and Korea, was worthy to pray to *The God of Heaven, The Supreme God* [8.] We now use the same name of *our God* [8] that our ancient ancestors used in primitive times. Before that decree, *all* of China, and *all* in this land," Kyung Jae emphasizes his words, "were *always* able to freely pray to *The Great*

8. *Hananim.*

One—the God of both *Korea* [9] and *China* [10]! Please, son, always remember that! It is so important. Some might want to convince you that some other god or religion is truly Korean. But you know. The Koreans and the Chinese both used the same name for that Supreme Being, in their own languages." "Kyung Jae repeats for emphasis, "Son, this happened in ancient times. A ver-r-r-ry long time ago!"

Young Kim now listens closely to every word that his father says. He wants to acknowledge his father's words without interrupting the thought. So, he says, "Yes, father, I know—'*Hananim*'."

"You know what happened when the two nations were abruptly deprived of a heavenly relationship." Kyung Jae says, a test of his son's logic. "Actually, they were deprived of a relationship with God Almighty." Kyung Jae hopes to hear his son echo his own inner thoughts. But Young Kim remained silent, only shaking his head.

A little frustrated, the elder farmer then shuffles his feet on the bank of the rice paddy and says, "Because of the Emperor of China, who also had influence over Korean matters, allowed only himself to pray to the God of Heaven, in all of both China and Korea, the people lost something of immeasurable value.

"Do you know what happened, Young Kim, when the people could no longer pray to the God of Heaven?" Kyung Jae prompts his son. He hopes to carefully instruct his son. His hope too, is to hear his son repeat the words that he, himself, is thinking in his own heart.

9. & 10 *Hananim* (9), and *Shang Di* (10); the same name for God used in primitive and contemporary Korea and China, respectively.

8

He mentally shakes his head at Young Kim's response of silence. So, Kyung Jae can only continue. He says, "The people's great sense of loss came because they were abruptly deprived of the deepest and most real relationship a human can have. A lost and broken relationship became Korea's and China's sad inheritance! What was taken from them was the right and the freedom to *freely* communicate with the Creator—their own Creator, and the Creator of the entire world!"

"Father, I think that would make my daily life so much emptier!" Young Kim says. It still seems somewhat abstract to him.

"Yes. The results are *very* logical, son," Kyung Jae says. He continues with bittersweet thoughtfulness, as he delights to relate highlights of Korean history. He continues, despite the pain elicited by the thought of the major tragedy in Korean—and world—history. Still, he hesitates, intending to bring the exact, needed emphasis to his words. "I am sure that what you said is just what our ancient ancestors felt, as well as the vast multitudes in China," his father adds.

"The people then began to hunger and thirst for something—*anything*— to fill that empty place, or as you said "the emptiness". But, that emptiness is not a simple loss of an activity 'no longer engaged in'. The loss manifested as truly an inner emptiness! The people lost their freedom, corporately and wholly, from being freely connected to the one who controlled the heavens, the earth, each individual's life, and the lives of everyone around them!

Young Kim continues to carefully listen.

"The people searched and were not satisfied until they found some other spiritual reality. They did find some comfort and peace in the religion of Buddha and the teachings and ways of Confucius" Kyung Jae says, with a parent's compassion. "And, naturally, a folk-religion began to develop, one that now is deeply rooted. That process is not uncommon in many parts of the world, especially in rural and isolated regions of the historic past! Yes, the Korean people sought a spiritual '*fix*'. Forgive me, if that word seems too casual. On the contrary, that slang word fits precisely," Young Kim's father soberly concludes.

Then, Kyung Jae begins to question his son with a hoped-for objective. "Tell me, how did the people search for the fix? *Folk-religion,*" he says, answering his own question. "That is the practice of spiritual *things* by those without spiritual *understanding*. A spiritual model has sprung up and developed in this country.

"*That* particular Korean, folk-religion has grown steadily through the ages. And, you have seen that many today falsely believe it to be the real and original spiritual discipline of this land."

Kyung Jae feels that the great impact of his monologue has reached its peak. "Son," he says with heartfelt conviction, "everyone—even all Koreans—would do well to learn of the deepest roots of our ancestors' spirituality. They would be so very happy if they knew that spirituality began with, and now is about the worship of the eternal God of heaven, '*Hananim*'.

"Okay, Young, now we must go to the field near the edge of the southeast hills. Do you see down there?" Kyung Jae asks with a wave of his muscular arm, as he now notices the field manager dealing with a labor-management need in the field. "There is some work being done there that I must attend to."

The two men begin to walk along the packed dirt bank alongside one rice field and leading toward another, where the field manager and workers are standing. As they walk, they savor the gradual increase of warmth the day offers. "Father, I hope this is not a distraction, but how can the people live, after having experienced such a ruinous loss in their lives?" Young Kim plaintively asks, feeling compassion for his ancestral, fellow-countrymen.

"That is a good question, Young Kim. Sometime after the relationship was severed, there came to these two countries a sound social order. A substitute system was adopted in the absence of the Great One/*Hananim*, Young," Kyung Jae answers, with an almost sentimental sound. "It was a system in place of the One with whom they had shared a trust and reliance."

With these words, Young Kim gazes at his father's eyes, which he otherwise would always avoid from respect, according to Korean tradition. Only now, and with difficulty, he tries to maintain eye contact, as the two walk rapidly, with little restraint. His father's eyes are like deep, dark, pools, unfathomable, but glittering with light. He savors this teachable moment. Out of a sense of awe and respect, Young Kim does not speak.

Both men are unified in their realization of the radical change that their homeland has undergone; and of an overshadowing change that had come thousands of years before.

Neither man moves now, nor speaks.

When the silence becomes substantial Kyung Jae slowly speaks, saying, "During the Han kingdom of our history, Confucian thought and the Buddhist religion were well established. However, the people needed more than the strong social order of Confucianism, which did not adequately fill the real void that had been left within them, since long before. Inwardly, they needed spiritual nurture, which was still to be found. All of China, and our ancestors lived for centuries having forgotten the true peace and security of a relationship with '*Hananim*'."

"Young Kim, I hope that you never forget that we are talking about the eternal, true and living Deity of this great land. No— better still, *I am talking of the Great Deity of the Universe! He was the Deity of this land, and its people long before any other deity, spirit-power or social institution was brought here or introduced as the replacement,*" Kyung Jae says emotionally, with strong emphasis. "Do you know that the name of our original Deity was not spoken or heard on the lips of a great number of the citizens under the Buddhist government, the later Confucian government, or even during the extended power and structure of the Yi dynasty? It was a spiritual tyranny!"

Kyung Jae looks down and then kicks at the dirt a couple of times, raising small clouds of dust with his shoe, and resumes his walk along the bank of the rice paddy with Young Kim next to him. His 'history lesson-homiletic' combination completes the instruction.

"Young Kim, just as our ancient ancestors once had direct access to heaven, likewise our Volunteer-labor Associations had relatively uncorrupted origins," his husky father says. Then, he stops, stoops and brushes dirt from the cuff of the leg of his traditional, all-white clothing. He often wears these rural clothes to remind himself of the rich inheritance that he and the country enjoy. It helps him to remember his inheritance of the divine gift of rightly-used tradition. Moreover, these clothes are a symbol for him and a hope-filled reminder of his constant prayer and deep hunger that the two Koreas would once again become one.

Kyung Jae hears an unexpected shout from the field, causing his attention and gaze to be directed not too far ahead of where he and Young Kim are walking. Then, he acknowledges the man, the field manager, with a wave of his arms. Kyung Jae and Young Kim continue to walk toward from where the shout had come. Quickly, they arrive at the place on the path directly across from where a group of workers stand in the field. Kyung Jae totally looks like the traditional farmer in the field; and he is more recognizable in the white clothes with his strong profile. He bends to roll up his pant legs, then wades through the shallow water, covered with nearly harvest-ready rice and thinks to remind his son of the reason he often prefers traditional clothing.

The farm cooperative leader quickly thinks that, for the benefit of everyone, later he will let his son's best friend help clarify the meaning of when the two Koreas were once one. As he wades into the rice field, he surveys the activity around him. He is about calf-deep in water as he arrives at the place to meet the field manager.

Kyung Jae and the workers in the field don't talk too long. But, he soon returns to the path near Young Kim, and says, "Let's go, quickly! It is time to go to the volunteer-labor *farm office* [11] now." Immediately, the two men turn and begin to walk. "Let's fully use this reclaimed gift of Christ-like living—in the Korean way! To live as He lived, to use a metaphor in the context of farm life, is like a healthy thoroughbred horse which must exercise

11. *nong chong*

its strength, *fully*, to realize its true potential as a highly valued horse.

"Also, Young, ours is a lifestyle of sacrificial giving. We *must* give, to bless our community," Kyung Jae says. "Whereas a valuable horse is able to simply live its life by its animal instinct, we humans do not live by instinct, as they do. We can, do and must make moral choices." The men continue to walk along the rice field engaged in edifying conversation."

"Young Kim, the horse's beauty is legendary among all animals. The horse is elegant and dynamic in its beauty. Its pleasing looks bring great satisfaction to its owner. The trainer must regularly give exercise to the thoroughbred horse to maintain its optimum form and health. If the trainer fails in the discipline, then a complete factor of the horse's being and value will be lost. Then, its value is much less than it may have been."

Again, Kyung Jae has begun to speak in metaphors since he knows that he and his son enjoy communicating on that level. Both men feel they are helped by the imagery of word-pictures. The leader of the farmers' group continues his analogy, "A magnificent horse has the potential to provide its owner with happiness—with real and deep joy! So, too, are gifts given to us from heaven, when used the right way."

Young Kim listens closely, hoping to absorb pearls of wisdom. Then he speaks, saying, "I know your words are true, father. I can see your word picture in my mind; still, I lack a real sense of the point. Can you clarify for me? There are good horses and . . ." Young Kim does not complete his thought, but he searches deeper, "Please give me an example of what our Volunteer-labor, farm life was like before there was 'Specialized Farmers'

Music. I know it seems unrelated, but I have recently been thinking of a few other music forms."

"I will do that. Then you will be able to see with your eyes open wide. And, I hope you will also be able to more intimately know the One who has handed you this 'torch of correctly-employed tradition'.

"Son, I love you, very much," his father says. "You are also well appreciated by the people of our village." With this, Young Kim's father holds steady eye contact and says, "I know that even some in the nearest city know about your abilities. You sing in the afternoon with he workers, and by *you* and by *that* they are very encouraged! You have earned respect. And, I must tell you that my respect is part of that total. Why? It is because you hold dear to yourself the good and true values—exactly as many of our ancestors have done, since so very long ago." Kyung Jae sees uncommon affection and tender openness emerging from within his heart.

Young Kim's face becomes flushed with both embarrassment and excitement, by his enjoyment of hearing these strong, complementary words. He thinks to himself, 'That *is* really great'!

"There! I see the farm office, father!" Young Kim announces, pointing, interrupting his semi-euphoric state. The men continue to walk and ease their way around the bend in the path that follows the base of the hillside. As they slow their pace, they soon stop near another scattered group of workers who are doing some pre-harvest weed clearing. The faint sound of a farm machine is heard from far across the field.

"Because the farm office is situated at the end of this hill, father, it reminds me of a big toe of the hill." Young Kim takes the chance to share a little word imagery. "The group has not arrived, yet, father," Young Kim says, as he looks at the farm office. "We may still see Ki Jun there." They approach the old unpainted structure which is made of weather-cured wood, but sturdy. The two men then complete their walk, happy as they advance the short distance to the office.

The field office is centrally located, and workers from farmhouses that surround it are more or less equidistant from it by foot. It is no more than just minutes away from any one of the homes. Still, it is empty when the men enter, and as they step in, onto the dirt floor, they feel comfortably at home.

Soon, they know by the sound of feet padding quickly and rhythmically on the footpath of the bank of the rice field that someone is approaching. The door quickly opens, and Ki Jun's smiling face greets the men, who offer a warm, friendly, "*Hello*"[12]. He bows before Kyung Jae and the men return the bow. Ki Jun follows Young Kim in leadership of the Farmers Music band, and is Young Kim's closest friend. The two young men spend much time in contact on virtually a daily basis, while working to support the community, through their music. They are, thus, very familiar with one another's personality, habits and character traits.

Ki Jun is the lead *small gong* [13] player. He plays the kind of gong that has a deep sound. It sings out notes that command the rhythm of the band. Ki Jun excels as the first small gong player, thus, he inspires the band mem-

---

12. *Annyong Haseyo*, Hello; the common Korean greeting-an equivalent of 'Shalom', or 'total well-being to you'. It may be used at all times.

13. *kwaenggwari*

bers. Accordingly, the band plays excellent music with excellent dance. They do work-service in the field. Ki Jun is very adept when he leads the band with the small gong's sonorous ring. As he begins to speak, a distant sound resounds suddenly across the rice paddies, like the thunder of metal.

The men then hear a shout, and Ki Jun spontaneously calls back through the window to the men in the field, who are within hearing distance. Then, he quickly turns and runs out through the doorway, onto the path, as Kyung Jae and Young Kim hurry to the window to rapidly see and locate the source of the scream. From outside, Ki Jun quickly stops, turns and shouts back, "Oh! Kyung Jae, Young Kim, there has been an accident on the road! It seems like something happened to a cart from the next village."

"What do you think happened, and to whom, father?" Young Kim asks a hurried question. He knows that his father is more familiar with the neighboring village than he is. "Could it be someone we know?" Young Kim says, almost whispering. "I do not know!" his father answers. "Could it be the Group of Specialized Farmers, on the road?" Young Kim persists, to complete his series of questions.

Now, Kyung Jae and Young Kim hear the sound of some men running and then watch the runners quickly pass the office, and proceed toward the site of the collision on the road. Their feet rhythmically pad the ground as they go, just as Ki Jun's had done earlier. The runners consist of a group of young men from the village's security and emergency team. Almost instantly they assembled by the nearby cluster of houses when they heard the noise of the accident, and quickly and efficiently they

now move a couple of hundred yards along the banks of
the fields of mature rice to the emergency.

At this time, Young Kim has lost all sense of compassion, despite the grave, dramatic impact and unexpected
suddenness of the accident. He *is* ironically anticipatory
and excited about the presence of the Group of Strolling
Actors [14] that he assumes is now close to Suwon-san.

Again, Ki Jun's face appears at the door of the office,
his usual wide and bright smile now less apparent. "*Yea*,
they are here!" he shouts, still enthusiastically.

"Who is where?" Young Kim's responds.

"Who is where?" Ki Jun echoes to his best friend.
Then, both young men speak the phrase together and say,
"The Specialized Farmers Band[14] group is here". Young
Kim then realizes that he answered the question, at the
same instant that his friend answered it.

"Do you mean you have not heard about them?" Ki
Jun queried. Even though he was enthused, he sounded
like he did not believe the answer. "Yea. We have heard
that a Specialized Farmers' Music and dance group
could pass by our little village of Suwon-san," Young
Kim affirms to his fellow band member. "These are the
ones they call 'strolling minstrels', or 'wandering minstrels'—the Specialized Farmers Music' bands!" His
father nods his head in agreement and says, "Yes. Please
tell us what happened in the accident."

"They are passing through. But more!" Ki Jun almost
screams in excitement. "Listen to this! They have made
plans to have a couple of performances in the next village, for a fund-raising tour. I have just heard that outside,

---

14. *Namsadang p'ae*

by the road." Ki Jun does not realize he didn't answer the question Young Kim asked about the accident.

"Do they have something new that the village wants to see?" Kyung Jae asks Ki Jun. Abruptly, Young Kim adds, "Father, I have not forgotten much of what you have told me of the history of the 'Bands of Wandering Minstrels'.

"Would it benefit us at all to go to see them perform, father? Perhaps even for just a brief time?" Young Kim asks, in all untimeliness. "We might learn some music skills that we could use, here in Suwon-san."

Young Kim *now* questions his father, as he almost pleads. Earlier, he thought they might really enjoy the experience.

"O.K. Young Kim," his father answers, as he seems to 'give in'. "Perhaps we must go see for ourselves what the Specialized Farmers music is actually like. Then, you should have a clearer picture of that about which you speak. Also, you will have an in-person experience to see if your information and opinion about them is true. You will see and learn, personally. Let us talk briefly, and then I will talk to Ki Jun." With that, Ki Jun walks out the door and steps toward the direction of the earlier commotion.

Determined, Kyung Jae then looks across the room and catches his son's eyes. As he looks, he is aware that the so-called generation gap is virtually non-existent in relationships in his family. So, the elder member of the family decides to take advantage of the two decades of added experience and apply his knowledge of Korean history.

So, he says to Young Kim, "*Every* change in our culture throughout history has not *always* been positive for our people. You have seen how I sometimes strongly oppose the apparent injustice in the traditional, Korean, class system. You remember Korean history, that some particular occupations have been offensive to the governing class of people, don't you? They believed that the introduction of 'occupational ranks' would give value and status to what one does to support oneself. Then, everyone would more easily know what kind of person they would be dealing with. That was done with the strong belief that social reform in Korea would be the result.

"But, Young Kim," his father says with the wisdom of hindsight, "those reforms were intended for those thought to be 'occupationally misguided'. From long-past generations, some occupations were considered by the ruling elite to be 'sub-normal' in a social-spiritual sense. Some occupations were evaluated by the general ethic of the country, while others were offensive to the prevailing, Buddhist ethic."

"I'm a little unsure what you mean by a 'social-spiritual sense'. Could you provide some explanation about that, father?" Young Kim asks.

"Good question," Kyung Jae answers. He smiles and says, "This is an example. Hundreds of years ago, a man was working to support a family as a butcher. This man's occupation was evaluated and placed on the lowest level. Why? Because, at that time, the government leaders were primarily Buddhists. The Buddhist sect of the King and the royal government had many vegetarians who thought that killing any animal was immoral; that is, any animal able to feel or sense pain. Thus, to be a butcher was regarded as having one of several lowly and dishonored vocations.

"So, it was the group decision by which national honor was sustained and validated, to reform social levels according to occupation," Kyung Jae explains. "The security of our villages was placed under the authority of the group decision, as well. Groups were subject to the group decision, but any independent decision was made at the risk of the individual independent decision-makers, him or herself."

Now, Young Kim is 'tracking' with his father. "So, do I now ask what independent decisions have Specialized Farmers groups made?" Young Kim does ask. "That is another good question. First, the home has less value in the home-village to the independent decision makers, Young Kim," his father instructs him. "Contrarily, these professionals live by the rules of the road. Perhaps, Young Kim, theirs is the inheritance of the well-remembered *'Hwarang'*[15], as some say."

"Everyone knows that the *Hwarang* are famous, Young Kim. They began as multi-talented, poetic warriors, trained for battle. They were much like what Westerners would call 'knights in shining armor'. They fought, they played music, they wrote poetry, and they performed. They did not have the armor of the European knights. But, they were a creative group and were the forebears of the strolling minstrels that we know today."

Now the father changes the topic, and then says with emphasis, "Young, there is a word that can represent a

---

15. *Hwarang.* A select, multi-talented group, assembled centuries ago, as 'knights of Korea'. Originally, Buddhist-elite, multi-talented, respected poets, writers and singers, they were also trained to fight to defend the 'honor of the land'. Their ranks evolved into the entertainment world, and thus much of their original 'pure and noble' character and nature was lost.

great separation between the lifestyles of *Specialized* and *Ture*. It represents the difference of *the time* away from your home village; away from the ones you love, you have loved, and the ones who love you. It involves what one group *did not* choose. An example is that the bands like the one passing nearby our village once had homes like ours. Then, centuries ago, they left it all for a life of traveling—to other villages."

"The first step away from where one is nurtured and raised, and away from a rural, farm community, is not an easy step. These men left their homes for a life of entertaining. They are truly musical professionals, Young Kim."

To begin a story set aside for this specific occasion, Kyung Jae says, "Group decisions are also a national tradition here in our country, Korea. And, that value has served for the good of the larger group and for unity. Young Kim, it is even for the good of our whole nation. This is especially true when the people heard, and hear— as one person—the voice of instruction of their God, who is *our* God, *Hananim*."

"This group which has come near our village is formed by unique individuals. They are very gifted. And, some of their decisions have been individual ones. Their development seems to be more based upon individual choices—rather than group decisions. They made decisions in search of their quest for what they thought to be *freedom*."

"So, Young Kim," Kyung Jae says, "they left their homes for *more* of *what seemed to be* the more valiant, gifted and romantic life." Kyung Jae refers now to the Specialized Farmers music groups. "They left their homes for a life of traveling, and so much more. If one were to consider their values for a long term of time, those values would appear to be less life-fulfilling.

"Still, the strolling minstrels are widely accepted. They are so popular." With this, Kyung Jae almost loses his breath, now being filled with emotion. But, he is able to continue. "You see, the rejection and loss of the value of continual, close, others-focused relationships, as a foundational value, is what I believe caused the strolling minstrels to become a band, wandering, as if without a home," Kyung Jae says, now more aware and emotionally focused.

Young Kim quickly answers and says, "But father, the Specialized farmers group can have a home *wherever* they go. Don't you see *that?*"

"That *is* the way it seems, isn't it? They turned away from the place that *will not* be taken away from anyone who treasures it. It is the place of values that will last forever—if we do not reject the One who provides homes for all of us. This is very important to me, Young Kim.

"Why is it so important? Because it is part of Heaven's gift to us," Kyung Jae says. "Again, it is like the thoroughbred horse. They must have regular, disciplined exercise, or they will not totally fulfill their roles as creatures of beauty, strength and majestic grace.

Now, Kyung Jae sits down to rest his large-framed body. "People exercise and horses exercise. Clearly, they do that in many very different ways," he says.

"Horses sometimes live in—what I will call a *wilderness*," Kyung Jae says, hoping to engage his son's keen interest in metaphors. "They can live either in captivity, or they can live in other ways. In most circumstances they were created with the capacity to be beautiful, magnificent animals," Kyung Jae says.

"Now, there are special kinds of horses. Some breeds of horses have a greater potential for running fast, like the wind. These would be race horses. Or, horses that jump or run a course. Some can do amazing things, for competition, for show, or for war—such as feats of strength, like pulling extremely heavy weights!" Kyung Jae exclaims to his son. "To people who see and enjoy them, these particular horses are more marvelous than the rest."

Young Kim now pays closer attention. "The people of whom we speak," his father continues, "are interested in that particular horse—and none other!"

His father shares a little of his somewhat-limited knowledge of the majestic animal and says, "Horses have characteristics of instinct that are peculiar to horses, just as all other types of animals each have their own instinctual characteristics. The horse is a beautiful animal among all animals. Toned and agile muscles characterize it as one of the larger animals. Even its mane and tail are beautiful to behold. And incidentally, as you know, the horsehair hat has a place in the fashion of the history of our great land.

"Yes, Young," his father adds, "horses have brought great practical fulfillment and pleasure to people throughout the world, for a very long time.

"Is it practical, too, when some people are not satisfied with living in one house, or remaining in one place, or even to own a home of their own, and they move to another place? Those people have the freedom and the right to live the way that they think is best.

Kyung Jae continues, "Those people, Young Kim, follow a different heritage than our heritage, which is this Volunteer Labor Community/*Ture*. Our life in this land has given us an opportunity to work in a special way and to produce food for our families. We do this with a special enthusiasm, Young.

"We have learned to interact with everyone in our village with the same, special, *unbiased* enthusiasm.

"Our village has a certain way of life," Kyung Jae explains. "We have the wonderful privilege to have proximity and relationship within our families," the elder community leader says to his son. "People throughout the world have that, also. Here in Suwon-san, we maintain close proximity and relationship with most all members of this community, as well."

"Good and healthy lifestyles will result in good and healthy relationships, Young Kim, almost without exception," Kyung Jae says, finalizing his point. "And, vice-versa. It is just like the animal's natural characteristics of beauty, strength, and its benefit to the environment; which would include the benefit to people. Therein, we witness full development. Do you follow the extent of this comparison?

"All families develop. That is a simple thought," Kyung Jae adds. "And, they may develop outside of the home!" he says. I might say 'exercising a family'.

"Marvelous horses, marvelous families!" Kyung Jae says, "That is the gift that we have inherited!"

"Yes, but father, people today say that self-determination proves the strength of one's individuality and self-will."

"That is my point, Young Kim. So often, we wake up, and at dawn we do our dance-march to the field. We also play our instruments and sing. This is an encouragement to—and a blessing for—the workers in the field. We sing songs of thanks for a plentiful harvest and for our good health. You and I know this, well. This is the way that our Volunteer-labor Farmers' Music and Dance Band begins its day. Isn't that correct, Young Kim?" his father asks him.

Both men become somewhat restless, since they have talked for such an extended time. So they begin to fidget and move around as they sit.

"Please remember something, before you answer. Sometimes, as we are going to do the day's work, your mother will be with many other farm women to cook for the time of celebration. The whole village joins in this kind of celebration. All the women from the village will talk together; they laugh and sing together, too. They do that while they all cook. They cook not just for their close friends or neighbors, but for everyone! That has been the tradition here, almost forever!" Kyung Jae does not want to let his son forget even part of his mother's vital contribution to community life. Then he smiles at his son, stands up, and puts his hand on his shoulder.

"Young Kim, we celebrate good things in life— everything good, in our home. Celebration times such as these are a necessary part of this life. Happily," Kyung Jae says, "we celebrate these things together."

"I understand that, father. It is something that makes life here so good!" Young Kim says enthusiastically. He *is* enthused, even as he thinks about the musical group that will soon perform in the next village.

"Celebration can be exercise!" the father enthuses. "Without consistent exercise, we may not gain the maximum potential. So, Young, we do our home exercises! Do you follow my thoughts, now?" he asks, with loving warmth.

"Of course I do," Young Kim answers a little defensively, still wanting to be seen by his father as a viable peer in the area of metaphor.

"Our family will grow closer and stronger, in our home. As the family gains and develops good values, so—as a horse is beautiful—we too can assimilate beauty, the beauty of goodness, Young Kim. Unique goodness!" Kyung Jae likes the metaphor. He also knows that he has reached the limit—again, and he laughs!

"In summary, I have learned that right living is our inheritance. Centuries of time have proven that the tradition of volunteer-labor on Korean farms can be economically sound and socially remarkable. There is one important thing that is essential in this system. This one thing must *never* be lacking."

"I know what the essential thing is, father," Young Kim volunteers, with enthusiasm. He guesses how he thinks his father would answer. "Our village's large banner, which is waving in the field, tells us about it! It says that farming is the divine gift, and that our Farmers' music and dance is also a gift that helps us to worship the Lord, and to farm in a more excellent way. And, father, the one, essential thing is that we *always* acknowledge the Divine Gift Giver—"*always, without exception*—and with joyful music and the praise due Him," Young Kim repeats for emphasis and clarity.

"Yes, excellent! It tells of our hope for a good future. And to remember and appreciate what we have, and from where it has come," confirmed his father. "Without that reminder and acknowledgment, we might be like any other village—even like a village in the north, where, regrettably, it is a totalitarian, anti-God regime.

"To actively be someone who lets others join with you in the living of a good life is an additional form of good exercise. Do you now more clearly see the value of exercise—and the parallels it has in life, Young Kim?" Kyung Jae asks. He has gone to great lengths to explain a concept that did not need such extensive talk, being mindful that they both enjoy the verbal play of metaphor and parallels.

Kyung Jae wants his son always to appreciate the great life-value, the joy, and the true hope in their redeemed, volunteer-labor lifestyle. They must have a right relationship with the God of creation; the God of their own individual selves. They are blessed to be gifted, and their decisions are also a gift inherited from individual ancestors.

Kyung Jae also thinks that life is best when a family is spiritually unified, it works together, and is happy and rested doing it! He thinks to himself, 'This *really* is awesome!' Kyung Jae actually feels deep gratitude in his heart that he and his son have many years of shared experience, doing what they so dearly love to do. 'That *is* fulfillment', and inwardly he smiles warmly.

He thinks, 'Surely, my son must be beginning to understand and know how uncommonly good this life can be, and is—especially when together, a community works for, and stands for truth in life. There is no life-style like this one!' So, he is eager to let his son grasp hold of that significant truth, and even help him, if necessary. It *is* a divine gift, he realizes once again. He would share that fact with the entire country, if he could!

Autumn weather is slowly approaching, and many young people are especially excited when they think of the coming days of the annual, national celebration of

'*Harvest day*' in the village. This occasion has been very much on Kyung Jae's mind, almost constantly! Now, that thought is becoming more active.

However, his son brings him back from his 'thought-state' when he says, questioning, "Father, I understand that there is strength and unity in the Asian way of group decision-making. Do you believe that the individualism of the strolling actors makes them non-productive and non-creative?"

"Young Kim, individualism in the farmers music community has produced new forms of entertainment," his father answers, placing emphasis on the positive aspect of the groups' contribution.

"The Strolling Actors are known and appreciated for some of their innovative and entertaining practices. Please, let this be an alert to you!"

"Some, but not all of the practices, father?" he asks.

"Yes." His father answers—with some restraint. "That which is unique is not always that which is to be desired, Young. Let me explain. The volunteer-labor villages are a Korean tradition. There, the individual works for the good of all of the community. But, each person has a part in making decisions. Although all may be equal, I know of no other lifestyle that is as fulfilling as the lifestyle here, in our village, which is dedicated to the Lord's work. You know how I dearly love the life that *Hananim* has given us," he says this as he looks out the window of the farm office at the rural landscape, which continues to slowly warm as the sun climbs in the sky.

Still distracted, Young Kim asks, "Father, if this discussion is complete, may I ask Ki Jun to enter?"

"Yes, Young, but I would like to take this opportunity to say just one more thing. Our family and our village have inherited some unique things, too. The disciplines, agricultural practices and social-spiritual relationships in our lives are truly unique. They are unique due to their excellent quality. We continue to practice them; they are patterned after Godly patterns. It contributes to the strength and growth of our country. That, my son, is irreplaceable.

"We receive much from this lifestyle," says the elder farmer. "The traveling minstrels, whom you will soon see, are not rewarded—by any means—the way that we are rewarded. No, I think not even if it seems to be so!" Kyung Jae takes a deep breath, and then finishes by saying, "Young Kim, if you will allow it, just what I am saying will be proven to you." Then, the farmer, wise for his years, stands and reaches to open the door for his son. Young Kim bows and turns to go to bring Ki Jun into the farm office. His father returns the bow, slowly—and thereby is able to conceal his misty eyes.

CHAPTER II

HISTORY IS MADE AT THE FIELD OFFICE

M oments after Ki Jun enters the office, Kyung Jae begins to talk very seriously. He is hoping for an objective equilibrium, so he will not be, or sound like a *didactic* model for the young man. Yet, his goal is to impress and impact the heart of his son's best friend and fellow band member.

So, he says, "Ki Jun, the Volunteer-labor Farmers Music Groups have great abilities, and, very often, they have times of laughter together. You know that." Kyung

Jae pauses then says, "I'm not sure if you know if my son, Young Kim, knows what I am telling you. It may interest you that he does, or does not. But, I will continue. The Volunteer-labor Farmers Music Groups have maintained and possessed our homes and our land for so many generations, and they have maintained our families for that length of time, too. All of that is for the good of community-bonding and togetherness, at least. The bonding serves for many things. It serves for much more than our personal, musical enjoyment."

Kyung Jae wants to clarify his point, so he concludes by saying, very soberly and slowly, *"Volunteer-labor life that is redeemed of the LORD* produces communities of *good living."*

"Yes," Ki Jun answers freely. His response sounds somewhat patronizing, since Ki Jun does not clearly understand what Kyung Jae wants to teach him. Like his best friend, his heart is distracted by the report of and knowledge that the Specialized Farmers Music Group is near Suwon-san. Almost everyone in the village is waiting expectantly for them to pass through the village, and many of the younger ones are running to the road to watch out for them—since the accident happened.

Ki Jun is also becoming excited to see them. He too, is actively anticipating what they will do. Earlier, Young Kim heard some related stories. He told Ki Jun as they met outside the farm office, "I will go now to the place where the accident occurred." It has been many minutes since they heard the noise of the accident, when Kyung Jae stood and watched his son as he left the farm office to turn and go in the direction of the road.

As he watched Young Kim hurry away, Kyung Jae was not unnecessarily anxious about the accident. He knows that a responsible emergency crew would quickly attend to this unusual occurrence on the main road. He remembers how he heard the crew moving so efficiently toward the scene of the accident, immediately after the sounds were heard.

To get re-focused now, Kyung Jae continues to tell Ki Jun what he wants so badly to say to him and his generation. He cannot let these ideas and truths go unspoken any more. He speaks with compassion, as if he were still talking to his son, and he continues from where he had completed his ideas. He knows that the two young men have many ideas and ideals in common. And, significantly, they share many personality traits.

The father knows that he can talk to his son and his son's closest co-worker-friend without withholding his true feelings and deepest emotions.

Ki Jun overheard some of the preceding conversation of the father and son—so both he and Kyung Jae know he will easily understand what he would say. "Specialized farmers music of today would not exist without the earlier formation and development of Volunteer, or Common-labor Farmers Music.

"The strolling minstrel music and performance was formed *much from the model of the Common-labor Farmers music*," Kyung Jae emphasizes, and now sees this as a good time to introduce his wife's message.

"Ki Jun, Common-labor Farmers music was created by many causes, for many reasons, and with many purposes," Young Kim's father says in a gentle voice, as he wants to communicate directly to Ki Jun's heart. Now, with his mind more focused, Kyung Jae wants the young man to be comfortable and offers him a place to sit.

"Please understand this, though you already know about *some* of this — as I said, the lifestyle of volunteer-labor associations is to live for the benefit of others, as well as for ourselves. As a village, we are strong. As we help the weak ones, we help the Great One, and the Great One is helping us — more and more — to do what we do."

"We have not learned to satisfy ourselves, only. Our success is based upon principles, including the important principle of equity. Do you know that each widow in this village receives care from her neighbors whenever necessary? We care for her, just as we care for someone like Mr. Yi, who owns the largest farm. And, often, more. We do not neglect him, either, though he is more able to care for his personal needs."

To draw another analogy, Kyung Jae continues, "Our reconciled, Volunteer-labor Association fulfills us, whereas the lifestyle of the North wants only to satisfy itself, ideally, and we know that does not fulfill. The famous Western scientist Albert Einstein, the "$E=MC^2$ man", even said that only a life of service to others is a life worth living! It is more than a matter of a difference in words. Why? We have been *given* direction. We have been *given* a healthy village. Although it may be gratifying, the strolling musician bands have inherited a *very* difficult way of life.

"*Isn't decadence an* applicable word, now? It seems to be the hidden inheritance, behind the more visible beautiful talents of music, acting, juggling, acrobatics, and even of travel," Kyung Jae proclaims.

"I believe that farmers music is beautiful, and the strolling minstrels are gifted players. My heart cries out for them! But, there is so much more than that. We would like to see them live a life which would offer them more purposeful and fulfilling lives. We believe there is so much more in this life for them."

Kyung Jae now adds a strong finish to the message, with hopeful expectancy. He says, "Even the North would accept folk-religionist, farmer-music-performers as equals—*if* they would serve the whole village! By serving the village, they would also serve Korea! Please consider these words, Ki Jun. I strongly believe this is more than my sentiment or emotion.

"An enhanced purpose would make *reconciliation*[1] with the North an easier thing and even some ideals of the North would find more people to receive fulfillment. These musicians would be better able to recognize true peace and true liberty, much like that which existed thousands of years ago, when our people were free to pray to the God of Heaven/*Hananim*."

"Specialized Farmers Music and Dance is bestowed with an inheritance. That *unseen* inheritance seems to be something like a new and aggressive, military thinking, which may produce divisions within its ranks."

"That may be analogous to the Communist regime of the North, which brought about an enmity in our land." Kyung Jae becomes emotional. "They rejected their own family and people for 'new' ideas and 'new' answers. They found a human philosophy to *attempt* to soothe their discontent, at a very great cost. Yet, volunteer-labor associations continue in many of the traditional ways," Kyung Jae says, with emphasis on 'the traditional'.

"But, those ways are *not* old-fashioned and lifeless, as some say. Rather, those ways are a model for successful

---

1. *tongil, Reunification;* the word of hope used by millions in separated families and the political arena.

reconciliation." Kyung Jae says. "Why? It welcomes *all* to work together—exceptionally voluntarily—not by force or compulsion, Ki Jun, *which* is another important and critical difference between our lifestyle and that of any repressive regime.

"We are the people of the God of Heaven. We are His family, and we cannot successfully act independently of Him, or even act independently of one another." Kyung Jae speaks these words of wisdom from his experience.

"The family of the God of Heaven/*Hananim* is a family meant to be united, not divided." Kyung Jae begins to open his heart to Ki Jun as to nobody else other than his family. He says, "The communists believe they want the best for all, but they would destroy those who do not agree with their strategy to do it. That, we have clearly seen. That attitude of mind is totally contrary to ours, which should be like God's attitude."

"Ki Jun, I know that reunification is something which you greatly desire, just as Young Kim does, and I do," Kyung Jae states, simply. "All Korea wants to be unified. Please consider this as we go to see the performance of the specialized farmers band, later. I think that you will like what you see . . . but please think deeply about it. Think very deeply."

At this point, Ki Jun notices that he is accepting Young Kim's father's thoughts—enough to let them have a place in his mind. His excited anticipation and openness for what he would see later, the specialized music, is cooled only a little by Kyung Jae's timely and emphatic words to him.

Ki Jun begins to think about sharing knowledge with Young Kim, precisely according to the latter's mother's plans.

Kyung Jae becomes more relaxed now, to continue the conversation, since he has communicated the message that his wife had requested. Now relieved, he says, "There is something very important, which is that Specialized farmers music of today does not exist as it is, simply because it is like the Volunteer-labor association Farmers music. No! Nor, does it exist as it is because we share similar values and goals. We know that we do not.

"That is an important fact, which may seem critical or proud. I believe that it is neither of those, Ki Jun. We have some time before we must go," Kyung Jae says, positioning himself closer to his son's friend, to help establish better trust, while also allowing him a clear view through the open office door. This farmer father knows very well about the magnetic attraction which specialized farmers music can, and does, have on the present generation.

"In the picture which the strolling performers are presenting to this generation, things are left behind. Some wholesome and productive things, even from the three Hans and three Kingdom dynasties."

"So, what is it that they have left?" Ki Jun asks.

"As you know, the word and even the concept of '*I*' is not a Farmers music principle. Neither is the principle of forced-labor—by threat, compulsion, or indoctrination. Oppression may seem good to those to whom the complete truth has not been given. But when a person learns the truth, then they are much more readily able to see what is untrue.

"Long ago, many, many centuries ago, bands were formed here in Korea. Specialized performing groups followed, in which the talent of the individual was supreme. However, the structure of Common-labor

Farmers Bands was not that way, with rare exceptions. It is not our Common-labor Association heritage." He hesitates and says, "If you will consider the differences, Ki Jun, you will see.

"Let me explain. First, in early Farmers band history, according to the 'new style', a team would go to village houses to play for the residents, and they received donations. Naturally, for them, the houses of the more affluent farmers were special places to go. Those farmers bands would play and do farmers music and dance. Soon, and increasingly, money motivated these times of performance."

Kyung Jae continues, "Then, as usual, with travel came *wear and tear*, and the bands had to buy new instruments, or repair their own. So there was an added need for income." He emphasizes, "*This was the beginning, financial stage for farmers music.* The age-old value of group priority and the all-inclusive group-identity of the Volunteer-labor Communities began to diminish from that time, forward. The time to *leave behind*, which I explained to you, follows after that."

"Before that time, members of village Common-labor groups had not worked for any specialized purpose—as special, professional musicians—separate from existing relationships in the village," Kyung Jae explains.

"Before this time, they did not leave the community to work independently, apart from the others. This is the first step by which they separated themselves from traditional Korea." Despite the sadness of this message, Kyung Jae speaks with a calm voice; firm, but low, and sensitive.

The farmer-father continues his talk to the gifted young musician, "In this stage of development, the band would leave their village of Common-labor membership and travel to other villages, Ki Jun—just as this specialized farmers band, which is traveling by our village today, is doing. As time passed and the bands traveled, they innovated, and they would do one or two new creative things to add to the attraction of their performance.

"Primarily, they would make house-call performances at the houses in *other* villages. Then, because they needed rice money and had other expenses, they would play in the marketplace. That is not impractical, is it?" Kyung Jae asks the young band member. Ki Jun answers, "No, sir." "Still", he continues, "these farmers groups became true money-makers. They became professionals. Nevertheless, they provided art and recreation," Kyung Jae says, completing his thought.

Then suddenly, he turns his head to look. Unexpectedly, Young Kim rushes through the open door, and excitedly interrupts the end of his father's lesson of farmers band tradition and history—something he has rarely ever done. Because of this, his father does not continue to talk, but waits.

"Oh! Father! Ki Jun! Hello." He bows quickly. Then, just as quickly, Young Kim begins to report, almost without breath. "The tragedy that happened was reported to me! They said that a cart with a group of orphans from the next village, and another cart of hopeful adoptive parents had an accident with a truck! Some were badly hurt and were taken to the hospital.

"Some people who saw the accident say that maybe several are in serious condition." Young Kim breathes quickly now, to recover his breath. "Father, not long ago, weren't the professional musicians of the lowest regard in this country, just as the 'seven despicable professions'

are—like prostitutes or butchers? Isn't that correct,
father?" Young Kim awkwardly questions his father for
confirmation.

"Yes, you are correct, Young Kim. Now, I will be
able to explain to you how these specialized farmers
music teams were able to join that group of people who
were not *just like* some of the *common people*[2].

Kyung Jae enjoys sharing Korean history so much
that he is now relaxed and moves closer to his son and
his son's friend—his cultural heirs. Despite the painful
content and context of these historical accounts, he
enjoys the value of his role in the preservation of national
history.

"I will continue from where I previously stopped.
Now, the second stage of professionalism and change
became what has been called 'the begging-rice troupe'
stage. It was also a way to earn money," Kyung Jae
says, feeling so thankful that he and his family are still
simply-and-surely, 'paid-for constituents', servants of
God, who are active members of and participating in a
Volunteer-labor Association. The attraction of individualism has grown and produced a collection of ones who
are independent individuals—and now the collection is
a group!" Kyung Jae exclaims, and is even impressed by
his last words.

"That was the result of social or moral practices
which were previously seen as objectionable by the
'national Korean mind', a *wholesome* mind. That was
the usual case, Young Kim," his father says, not fully
explaining about the ancient system of social-level dis-

2. *minjung.*

crimination, which even now still disappears only little-by-little in Korea.

"Do you think the performers of this specialized farmers band would still participate in the labor, as we do, and as was previously done?" Young Kim's father asked his son. He added, "Before you answer the question, truly consider about their new activities."

Young Kim thought for a few moments and looked at his father. "No, father, how could a Volunteer-labor Farmers Band both travel as professional musicians and work during labor times of the season," he begs.

"Yes, you do see! his father says. He is pleased by Young Kim's response. "There are definite and established times for transplanting, for weeding, and for harvesting. You are very correct, Young Kim! And while that band is at other villages performing for money, they will become skilled musicians. Do you agree with this idea, too?"

"Of course, father. These strolling minstrels of today are known for their musical and dramatic abilities; as well as the other things, as rope dancing and aerobatics. Others are noted for their mask-dance and clown play. That is why so many of the people like to see them perform, father," Young Kim tells his father what he knows of the strolling minstrels' great popularity among the youth of surrounding villages, and the city. "How can they be farmers, also?" he adds.

"Young Kim, you are our only son. Let me create an imagined story. Think of yourself as if you were Hong Jae. Imagine that he is your age and he has two brothers. Can you do that? Then, you may better understand how Farmers music was the offspring of the Volunteer-labor Farmers' Association lifestyle. I can also tell you how that child grew up and left his home and family," his father says, and prepares to make a realistic scenario for his son's understanding, and for his ethical convictions.

Across the room, Ki Jun turns and takes a bottle of water, from which he fills three ceramic cups. Then, he holds one out for Kyung Jae and the other to Young Kim. Then, he gulps the remaining cup of water, very rapidly, excuses himself, and returns to the position where he can again listen closely.

"Young, think of Hong Jae's father as the overall leader of the Common-labor Community. He has three sons who are men like you, 'Hong Jae'. They are also members of the Common-labor Group. Each of the three sons is a landowner, having a share in the Common-labor Association Labor pool.

"Do you follow the story, Young Kim?"

"Yes father, I'm fairly sure," Young Kim answers. "Hong Jae is the son of the leader, just as I am your son and you are the *overall community leader*[3]," Young Kim responds attentively, and cautiously.

"That's great! I am so glad that you understand, Young Kim," his father says, as he beams with a big smile.

"Now, the three sons have three positions in the Farmers Music Band. These three are like the three stages of Farmers music and dance, which I have just described to you. I will recount those stages. They are: first, the house-calling farmers music, then, the rice-begging troupe, and third, the troupe of strolling actors. Do you follow my thoughts, Young? And you, Ki Jun?"

3. Y*ongjwa*

Kyung Jae seeks to maintain the attention of the two young men on this subject, as this subject has much personal and historical value to him.

"I am following in the same footsteps that you have walked, father," answers Young Kim.

Ki Jun agrees with a quiet, "Yea!"

"Good." Kyung Jae is ready to continue. "So, each son is like an entire Common-labor Farmers Music Band, and each one decides to leave their father's leadership and the village. Each son has heard of the ways to make money, and how to become a professional musician. Each brother believes that he will find satisfaction and fulfillment by providing entertainment, music band talents, and by sharing that with their own countrymen, women and children." Kyung Jae draws the word-picture in more detail.

"The three sons, including Hong Jae, want very much to travel from village to village."

"And, they each want to learn what they can accomplish for themselves and for the sake of the culture of their homeland," he continues. "That is a very noble-sounding cause. The three sons are at a place in their lives that they must make an awkward choice.

"Each son has made the choice to depart for new territories and for new horizons," Kyung Jae says, beginning to bring his word-picture into focus.

"They represent the growth of farmers music as a new, independent agency. Still, they are the first sons to choose a different form of life than to fully support *the group*. They make a hard choice, to turn away from families, the home-band, the home-village, and hard work they were raised-up to do for the community's sake." Kyung Jae pauses to take a deep breath before he continues.

"The sons have chosen a 'new' lifestyle. Even while no other village member could quit the Volunteer-labor Association without a request and release from the village leaders. That was a proven way to keep unity strong and intact. They also turned away from advantages of Volunteer-labor—which hold many, great promises for the future—all for the sake of the other music and dance group members. However, these band members did not reject *redeemed* Volunteer-labor life. Why? The God of our ancient ancestors had not yet revealed the Lord and His truth to this nation, until hundreds of years later."

"The Specialized Farmers Band members have now become part of a 'movement', and chose not to be depended upon by, nor be accountable to, their own village, as they have been doing—for such a very long time." Kyung Jae concludes. Then, he breathes deeply and sighs. Because he relates history, not simply an intellectual exercise, but much more than that. He remembers that for centuries a bitter, bitter war raged over Korea—and he knew that he was one who had heard something to do that he could not refuse—the clear and distinct call to *take dominion* . . .

Now, he looks with open tenderness into his son's eyes. Young Kim catches and savors the look, then, self-consciously, embarrassed, and trying to be respectful, averts his eyes out through the open door, to the ripening rice fields. His gaze crosses the fields to near where the morning's event took place. He is still unable not to wonder about the involvement of the itinerant-farmers Music Band on the eastern road from Suwon-san.

Both men grow silent. Young Kim continues to stare a great distance away, more or less vacantly, across the rice paddy to the road. At the same time, his father draws thoughts from deep within. He thinks of Korea—both of today and what he has learned of the land of the ancient ancestors. Kyung Jae has always worked with his son with care and great joy, both as a father and a co-worker. He knows Young Kim is hard-working and dependable; a worker of good reputation in the community. The father's dream was that his son could help the village rise from the ashes—and thus help to restore, the practices and values of the ancient, national tradition of Volunteer-labor Farming, and its integral music and dance, whose original form has been all but lost.

So, the farmer-father begins to speak of that, "A restored order is a necessary element for completion of the lifestyle. No! I'll correct myself. The restored order must be foundational. It must be the discipline of living a life submitted to the God of our ancestors—our own God!

"Please listen, and understand, Young Kim. The Common-labor Farming life was radically suppressed during the Japanese occupation. Even the musical instruments of the Common-labor Farmers Music Bands were confiscated, because they represented symbols of Korean national identity. That identity hindered the Japanese goal of re-identifying Korea exclusively with Japan.

"But, I will tell you a side note; a very important, and necessary thing, though it takes me off the subject. Young Kim and Ki Jun, we must never forget that the Japanese occupation is a *past* tragedy. Yes, it was so severe. We have forgiven, and must always forgive, and bless! The historical, Korean battle is one against spiritual powers and forces—not against the Japanese, or any people. Please always remember that!

"Let me continue. The original, ancient cycle of shared labor had also been broken by innovations in field irrigation. How do we know that?" Kyung Jae asked his son and immediately answered, "Chinese records show that rice farming began to be done in Korea in the year 33 A.D. An interesting and decisive year of history, isn't it? This was the time of the Three Kingdoms period. Even then, the records told of rice farming, with the aid of irrigation."

"In those days so long ago, there was a division in the labor force," Kyung Jae again enjoys more and more recounting accounts of his homeland, which has withstood so much. *"The class of nobles and aristocrats* [4] at this time began to be *excepted* from taking part in the Common-labor Cooperatives in the villages. These men of position did not have to serve, nor work. Young Kim and Ki Jun," Kyung Jae takes another deep breath. He continues, saying, "At that time, there was a need for intensive labor for irrigation in the rice fields. Volunteer or Common-labor teams were-well suited to accomplish that task, and individual farmers were not successfully able to accomplish it, by themselves only. The change came first in irrigation practices within the Common-labor Associations."

"Then," Kyung Jae quickly adds, "after the development of Volunteer-labor Farmers music, the farmers music itself began to pass through a process of change.

---

4. Y*angban*, a term originally reserved for the intellectual elite—historically, a group of career, government officials who obtained their posts by excelling on a government exam.

There were diverse characteristics involved in both Volunteer-labor farmers music and other farmers music, not identified with Volunteer-labor Associations. That helped to make the two farmers' music systems recognizable almost as one music form. The nature of one form was tied-up inherently in its lifestyle. That of the other was not."

Thus, the dream that Young Kim's father dreamed was one of seeing at least the partial restoration of a system and a lifestyle, in which every person in the village would receive benefit—both justly and fairly. He would once again like to see the strength of total commitment by each and every village member. He knew by experience that the good results of such a commitment were not surpassed anywhere that he, or anyone he knew, was aware of.

"*Nobody* is neglected in a Redeemed, Voluntary, Common-labor Association village which is administrated responsibly. Every widow, the sick, and the weak are always given adequate benefits, according to their needs, through donated labor to the village," he says, making his point clear.

Not the nostalgic type, nor a pragmatist, still Kyung Jae values things which help keep the family strong— despite the rapidly changing, 'cultural climate' of his homeland - which is now becoming 'Westernized'. For Kyung Jae, this was and is a tested way to live a wholesome life. His parents lived the traditional Volunteer-labor Association lifestyle. But, they too were considered 'Westernized' due to their alleged adherence to what many naively considered to be non-traditional religion. Moreover, they were part of the rare presence of the volunteer-labor groups, which had virtually disappeared during the Japanese colonial rule.

For centuries, Confucianism was the predominant thought among the powerful noblemen/government—officials. Buddhism had also been the official state religion in Korea during the reign of various generations of kings.

After he spoke to his son and his son's best friend, Kyung Jae paused to ponder this knowledge at length, and once again begins to speak to Young Kim, who is now more alert and responsive. As he waits, members of the Common-labor Association's group begin to come into the Association's office, and after a brief stay, each one leaves in the order they entered. These men are beginning to actively make preparations for a meeting planned for that day in the office.

Despite the office's small size, the father and son still continue their meaningful conversation without being distracted, or interrupted. "My son, do you remember the earlier word picture in which we shared of the oldest brother of Hong Jae?" asks the father. "He is the son who was most active, when he departed from his family's way of life. His departure was of greater importance than that of the other brothers. But he was able to do that with the aid of his two younger brothers. The brothers enabled the older one to go beyond the place which he, and they, had ever gone in finding freedom to do what he wanted to do—independent of the group decision. They could be called the specialized farmers-music pioneers.

"Without his two brothers, perhaps the older brother would not have walked the path that he did," Kyung Jae adds. "The older brother was the one who became the most specialized and the most professional. He also was the one who was joined by the greatest number of others in the group. In that way, he became the leader of a very big band of professionals. He exercised great influence upon almost everyone around him.

"In the story, he is now with a troupe of strolling minstrels and actors, Young Kim," his father says. "The older brother is like a symbol of the group which is passing by Suwon-san today. He is a type of one of the 'Specialized Farmers Music and Dance', which go from market to market and from village to village to perform. They are not limited to farmers music and dance. They have also done what is very much unlike farmers music." Kyung Jae begins to build the details of history in his mind to relate to his son.

Again, Kyung Jae begins and says, "The group that is passing our village is not a small group," he stops to catch his breath, draws a deep breath and begins to talk more methodically. "They have accumulated a number of entertainers which have been added to their '*non*-common-labor association farmers music, over the years. And, as you know young Kim, these newer additions have diverse talents.

"Yes, they are true entertainers, father," replies Young Kim. "We have what is necessary to accomplish our work through the Common-labor Farmers Music Band of our village," explains Kyung Jae. "And, it is good and very necessary that we also have what is needed to engage in joyful times of celebrating and village dancing. All of us, *everyone*, takes part. Isn't that right, son?"

"Father, you know that we always participate together. And we are always filled with happiness and joy."

"Now," Kyung Jae quickly continues, "the elder son once lived just as we do. He then became unhappy with living a simple life—unhappy being dependent upon others for mutual fulfillment in the life of that village, and not happy with others depending upon him in a committed way. With responsibility often comes emotional pressure. This older brother wanted to be released from the pressure.

"The committed, systematic and cooperative actions of the Volunteer-labor association lost its appeal in favor of the idea of independent action, my dear son," Young Kim's father says, now tenderly. "So, what did he do? He collected his musical instrument and his clothes for dancing and celebrations, and searched for others who were of a similar mind," Kyung Jae says, beginning to bring his analogy to a close.

"This gifted man joined others like him, and as a band member, he began to tour the villages, and go from marketplace to marketplace. Soon, he saw that the other band members were gifted individuals who were applying their talents to new and exciting performance activities. You know of these talents and activities, Young Kim. Don't you?"

After his son's affirmative response, Kyung Jae begins to build details of another segment of history in his mind to effectively relate to him. He continues and repeats his earlier words, "The group that is passing our village is not a small group." He stops now, and waits to see if his son notices his intentional, redundant repetition of the statement.

Just as Kyung Jae begins to speak again, Young Kim speaks first and says, "Yes, father, every teenager and college age person loves to talk about the *nongak*[5] band members. *Very many* would like to join Farmers Music Bands. They would like to find the freedom and the stimulating life, which they see in Farmers Music Bands. Of course, you know that I mean the kind of band that travels and performs.

"Father, you must know of some tightrope dancers who are such good actors and who can make the people laugh?" Young Kim asks, to actively involve his father in his own 'new special-interest'. "Yes, they amuse and entertain the people of every town and village, just as their companions do." Kyung Jae answers, to show his desire to be on track together with his son.

Even this slight mention of 'exotic' performers serves to stimulate the younger farmer-musician, although this is not the father's intended result. Still, this talk excites Young Kim, typical of most anyone his age, throughout the land.

"May I continue the story, Young Kim?" Kyung Jae immediately asks. He begins with a brief pause for Young Kim's answer, "The independent farmers music band with which the elder son involved himself, was a group of diversely talented people. They added people with abilities that traditional Farmers Band had previously never used. This group's actions resulted in them being separated from all involvement with the people of their own village.

"Young Kim, people know that is a typical necessity in life to support oneself. But, with the unique history of this land and this people, we do—and must—live *beyond* what is commonly thought practical. Now, as farmer

---

5. Farmers music and dance

band members begin to no longer desire to be part of, or be treated as a part of the permanent local community, so the professional, itinerant genre develops. The younger man sits amazed now, to hear this historical truth communicated to him by his own father. "This group eventually becomes what we call in our language, *namsadang p'ae* [6]. They did not think with the priority of orientation and decisions; and so they no longer re-generate as previously; no longer a presence in the village, continuously and for the common good."

"Even since the time of the Japanese occupation, for the first time the first Farmers Music Groups began to receive pay as individuals," the elder man says, sounding unusually like an intellectual. He is not bitter, but objective in intent. "First, Young Kim, before changes of structure began in this lifestyle, initial payouts went exclusively to fund needs, which were common to each village, individually. Individuals would not be personally paid for labor. But, today that is no longer the case.

"As I have mentioned, there are now tight rope dancers, acrobatic performers, mask dance players, clown players, saucer spinners—and even more—to amuse and entertain the people of every town and village," the father says, desiring to confirm common knowledge that he and his son share.

"Clearly, the youth talk much about the farmers-music life, simply because it appears so appealing," Kyung Jae says. This time he sounds like a teacher. "There is a part of the biography of the eldest son, about whom we have

---

6. Korean words for a 'group of professional musicians', a.k.a. 'group of strolling actors/wandering Minstrels/'S*pecialized F*armers Music and Dance'.

been speaking, that has not been exposed, nor understood by the youth of today. The unknown part of his life
is the youthful part."

He goes on to say, "After Volunteer-labor Associations
gave figurative 'birth' to the eldest son, of whom we
have made a story, he, by himself, became the symbol of
the troupe of wandering actors. There was no biography
written which endured to reach the ears and hearts of the
people of the nation," the father says to the listening ears
of his very attentive son.

"The popularly known biography was recorded from
a recent point of view. It is a point of view that most
Koreans see today. It is the popular view of farmers
music, about which we always hear, son." He continues,
"The part of the biography in which the eldest son was
growing, is not well known. Young Kim, before we go
to the neighboring village to see the Specialized Farmers
Music and Dance, let me tell you the story about the
hidden biography of the beloved, eldest son."

Now Kyung Jae takes another deep breath, with the
expectation that his word picture will communicate clear
truth to his son. "When the son decided to leave the village, he sought and found a group that needed a lead
singer. He was invited, and invited himself, to join that
Farmers Music Group, and he joined the group. Then,
he began to travel with them, doing the rites and performances in many villages.

"Soon, Young Kim, the son realized his tradition
and its accompanying lifestyle—that of Volunteer-
labor Farmers music—from which he learned to sing in
response, no longer had a place that belonged in his life,"
Kyung Jae says. He takes another deep breath, pauses
and thinks. "He was not able to sing in the style to which

he was accustomed, now being with the group that performed in the villages and before crowds. Farm work was no longer involved. The group found another role, which the son was capable to play, and so his abilities were extended. I would say that those abilities became less 'pure'," Kyung Jae adds.

"The elder son in our story is therefore a multi-talented performer, representing the several abilities and arts of the group. While the group is growing in number and developing, performers come from various backgrounds. Some, like the eldest son, are discontent and are looking for 'a new and better way of life'.

"Try hard to understand this. This can help you with your musical interests. And, it is good that you know some background of what you will soon be seeing" he says.

"So, my son, Specialized farmers music sought every way within the bounds of professional music and entertainment to please the people."

Kyung Jae now becomes totally absorbed in relating more of his personal knowledge and experience to his son, whose generation lacks much direct knowledge or experience regarding the contrasts of the two kinds of "farmers bands".

He continues to tell his son that the itinerant musician-actors were truly professionals. "Please understand their goal. Of course, it is to remain professional. Let us look at the character of the son. As an independent thinker, the son is free to exercise his professional abilities, and for his own benefit. Of course, that is what everybody would say is natural in life."

Kyung Jae changes the subject abruptly, and reports, "Excuse this, and excuse me. But, I must abruptly make an important change in the direction of the conversation. Why? Because, I need to plan for the meeting with the leading elders of the neighboring village!"

"As you know, there are a significant number of children without parents in that village. This is very important to those of us in our village, in this country, and in the world, Young Kim." The father speaks soberly, and with little self-consciousness. "When we see them doing their acting and playing their music, we will be able to talk about working with them, to help them any way that we might.

"Excuse me again. That has been a serious concern of many for a very long time," Kyung Jae says. "It is still serious. Let me return to the subject. Even the temporary end of Common-labor Farm Associations in this land was a very sad thing, for we lost an important, Korean-born, socio-economic system, Young Kim. A legacy was lost. I have explained some of the many reasons that contributed to its decline. The history is long, and its beginning is from ancient history." Kyung Jae now becomes solemn, and talks as one who has just received confidential, legal testimony to support his case. That is, he is serious, but with a deep, inner confidence.

Kyung Jae knows well the fascination that the skilled, performing troupe holds in the minds of the younger generation. He addresses that issue. "The great attraction of Specialized Farmers Music is its independence, and, of course, that it is specialized. The performers developed and integrated a rite in which they continue to perform, the shamanistic-folk religion rituals, throughout the villages. But listen, Young Kim, there was a time that was so important in our nation's history related to those rites. May I explain about the farmers' rebellions in the Yi Dynasty?

"Close to the last century of the absolute monarchy of the 500 year Yi Dynasty, farmers were taxed double the previous amount." Kyung Jae says as he illuminates some related background. "That was in the 17th century."

"It was doubly difficult, also, as much of the tax money went to the king's advisors, who were among the aristocratic elite. Because of that, they were respected even less than before by the common man, and by the farmers, especially."

"At that time, farmers had developed a better way to cultivate rice, Young. This allowed each farmer to till and harvest more land. Due to this advance in irrigation technology, unfortunately, the need for labor decreased."

"And, do you know what happened on the farms?" His father asks.

"Did many workers become idle, father?" Young Kim guesses.

"That's right, absolutely, son!" He confirms the answer with 'philosophical intensity'. "There was a great amount of farm workers who were deprived of their customary work, even for decades. They were forced to become wanderers. Some turned to begging and others to robbery. What is important to know at this time is that many began to work doing the things that specialized farmers do now—even to this day! There was a necessity."

Kyung Jae then says, "Then, the Yi government began to consider the whole class of jobless farm workers as criminals, because of the minority. Beggars, robbers, and many others, those who were lazy and idle; these brought wholesale blame and disrepute upon a whole stratum of society. The real problem was with those who did not have the motivation to do very much in their lives.

"Some of the more creative and motivated ones joined the circus. They became clowns, actors, and circus entertainers. Still, the government did not treat them fairly, but treated them severely."

"Father, it is hard to believe that our government could have been so hard to its own citizens," Young Kim exclaims.

"Yes, it is greatly lamentable. The farmers continued to pay high taxes to the Yi government, and tens of thousands of farm workers were brought to the point of riots and rebellions against the Yi Dynasty," Kyung Jae reports. He feels that even with stinging, social upheavals that his son would learn from it and become a better patriot and a more effective loving contributor to the homeland.

Kyung Jae feels that although Western influence in Korea was strong, it was not necessarily all negative, or anti-Korean. But, he also feels that without that influence, the country would have eventually been overrun, from one source, or another. This was proof—if only to himself—that Kyung Jae was patriotic

"So, there were violent riots of great numbers of farmers over the decades during the Yi Dynasty," the patriotic musician-farmer continues.

"A planned and organized rebellion of vagabond farm workers almost ignited like a raging fire in the King's palace. It originated as rituals from their predecessors who were practiced in the arts of sorcery," reveals Kyung Jae. "These 'Flower Boys', also called "Flowering Youth' were very highly respected for the things for which they were best known—that is, as knights and gallant warriors. Their heritage began as certain gifted Buddhists who had the ethic of 'no righteousness in war'. Still, they developed a moral code.

"Honor, loyalty and truth were the hallmarks of this group of young, gifted, and valiant Koreans. As time passed, however, they were well known, but not for the other parts of their lives—of which history tells us," Young Kim's father shares yet more interesting facts from his memory of the history of the land.

"Later, a part of the group of the Flower Boys was the 'pretty boy'/*Hwarang*, from whom came the 'Strolling Minstrels'. They would sometimes dress in women's clothes—initially, to adhere to the acting form of the Far East of exclusively *male* actors. They worked also as traveling, male prostitutes," Kyung Jae now speaks, somewhat restrained. "Some say that it is from that tradition that the Specialized Farmers Music bands evolved. It did *not* evolve or come from the root—the Volunteer-labor Farmers music."

Now, Kyung Jae hesitates with the weight of the truth of his words. "It is not an easy thing to understand, or to reconcile in one's heart," Young Kim's knowledgeable father says, with compassion. He carefully avoids the tidal wave of further disclosure that may be considered a source of national shame. His son now sees that this man, his father, portrays and models humble gratefulness. That does not come inherently with his role and position in life, even as it comes with other roles that are less blessed.

Kyung Jae does not stop. He continues and says, "These are the ones who did not learn about the true dignity of man," he carefully explains to his son. "Our people did not fully understand that truth. The Confucian and Buddhist governments tried to grasp the idea, but were not able. It is not an Eastern way!"

"Only through the Great One, the true Creator of our nation—and of all things—did we, and our ancestors, come to learn the truth about our dignity as people. We are human, and we are Koreans. God, whom we call '*Hananim*', made us like Himself in His image.

"Young Kim, only humankind is like Him," his father says, as he looks boldly into his son's eyes. "Not any animal." To Kyung Jae, this truth about God is integrated into every aspect of real Volunteer-labor Farm life.

So, he continues, "And we must come together, work together, and remember that many bands and groups want to be patriotic, creative, Koreans. And they *are* that in their minds, though not always, in my opinion, in truth. They may do shaman rituals from ancient tradition, to bless the houses. They have made themselves to be professionals. They aren't quite like our early ancestors who established the basis of the spiritual life in Korea, and were true patriots!" Kyung Jae exclaims.

"If not, why not?" he answers while also asking himself.

"Because they seem unable to see far enough back into the past, or close enough now to see God, Who has always been there for us—and for everyone who calls on His name. And even now, He is here, still!" Kyung Jae now speaks with confident assurance.

Young Kim asks, "Why would someone leave a secure and happy life with co-operative, work-for-everyone, in-every-part-of-life—for the life of strolling minstrels?"

"Specialized Farmers Music is professional music and dance," his father responds. "Please do not think that I have any bias against professional music, even as a lower scale occupation, as it was established in the Yi dynasty. No. There is freedom to travel and freedom in social habits. But, patterns of amoral habits exist therewith, which by the values given to us by the God of our ancestors, do not fully acknowledge man's social dignity or human worth."

"Because of this, a significant part of why they are so popular is seen, son." Kyung Jae has completed his burden to share his heart, having thus said all that was necessary, for now.

"Father," Young Kim begins, while concepts and images of popular farmers music dance in his head . . . "Father," he repeats, now not feeling totally secure with the values that he was taught and has lived, "I see that the troupe of wandering actors has kept some appearance of the traditional things of the past. But they offer such depth and variety in their performances—and the people love them!" Young Kim says, clearly and visibly enthused.

"We can go together to the next village, where the people say they will perform," his father answers. "There, together, we can see what I have told you. There, *you* will be able to see if these professional entertainers follow in the steps of their predecessors from about two thousand years ago."

There, you can ask me any question you might have related to our lives and theirs. That may also help you see more clearly about the men from the neighbor village, too," Kyung Jae says.

"Yes, father," Young Kim agrees, still eager. "I would like to go and see, and learn more about real 'nongak', farmers music and dance, life," Young Kim answers, not effectively able to hide his enthusiasm and excitement for the anticipated band's popular and novel attraction.

CHAPTER III

WATER DOES NOT FLOW UPWARD

"**S**on, today you can enjoy the performance of the *Troupe of Strolling Actors*,[1]," Kyung Jae says. "Please," he said emphatically, "be reserved, and remain anonymous until we are ready to talk to the leader after the performance. Why? Then, we will have the opportunity to see the performance as another might see it—not only from our own point of view. Kyung Jae explains as

---

1. *Namsadang p'ae*

a father, and one experienced in life and music. That will allow us to be objective."

Young Kim agrees with his father, "That is good, father. For, I would prefer to see them perform as someone not having lived the *Volunteer-labor Association*[2] life. It will be interesting to learn if I can truly see differently.

"That's right," Kyung Jae answers his son. "Only try to stand away from the front line of people around the performance area. Then, they should not see you or me easily, son," counseled the man of a generation of more experience, as he stands to leave for the market.

As the two men leave the field office, they see others coming toward the office and others who are walking in the same direction, ahead of them.

They walk the path in the still-warming day along broad rice fields. As they approach the town, the Farmers Music Troupe of Strolling Actors has completed visits to certain houses in the village. They performed there, including doing some rites of over-coming evil spirits. They strategically chose the houses of the more prosperous landowners who would be better able to pay them more generously for their services.

Kyung Jae sees this practice as one clear distinction from his Common-labor association Farmers music tradition. He reflects on that idea to himself, and thinks of himself from a patriotic perspective. Again, Kyung Jae reflects as they approach the town's marketplace. There, he and Young Kim see the performance of the Specialized Farmers Music Band is about to begin.

"Our Common-labor association band has the welfare of the entire village in mind," Kyung Jae speaks

---

2. *Ture/Doorae*

his thought aloud to his son. "And the village, likewise, considers the Volunteer-labor Farmers Music Band as equals. As the band considers the various parts of the village—they consider all, *before* themselves!" Kyung Jae again drives his point home.

'I don't think so,' Young Kim thinks, 'the professional band wants to seek the most rewarding areas for profit for their work.' In contrast, the Volunteer-labor Community is 'community-focused', and group focused—it is *'others focused'*. The professional Farmers Music Group, separated and specialized, is focused on itself and its own skills; focused on the band, and finally, focused on the individual, or group of clients who pay for their services.

Despite some weaknesses, the professional music band gives a fine performance. Kyung Jae watches as the two tightrope dancers of the group repeatedly leap and perform daring and humorous antics high above the marketplace grounds. They have a charming ability to hold his attention, and even bring a smile to his lips. Still, he muses that all things considered, the Volunteer-labor Farmers music and dance is the true mother of all Farmers music and dance! The Specialized Farmers Music and Dance players have deserted and disowned that mother.

"This is *a process* in reverse!" Kyung Jae again vocalizes his thought. "It is as if 'the child has made an orphan of the mother'!" Kyung Jae thinks and feels his case is well made, now—maybe even too well.

'This 'oldest son' had developed his skills to a professional level', Kyung Jae thinks to himself. 'He has developed a lifestyle which is 'self-focused". And an afterthought, 'Even to the point of decadence! And again, since this was the inheritance, it would now determine the future of many others.'

Yet, today, in the year 1965, there is no clear or apparent evidence to the people's eyes, which could be argued for the case; nor did the traditional, respectful role of 'mother' matter to the professionals.

With that thought, Kyung Jae looks at his son and says, "Young Kim, as you watch this group, remember the place from which they began in the quest for their *independent* specialization. It is a different kind of growth process. Look, and you will see how they grew *away* from the values of the 'mother occupation'—that of *Common-labor Association Farmers music*, [3] and towards their own values. "Our vision is clear, son. But, I believe that their vision has prevented them from seeing the progression to the end state of their activities. Having said that, Kyung Jae begins to feel somewhat awkward, since he had been voicing his analysis between seeing the presentation of some daring acts of aerial feats.

"Then see, if you will, the heart of this group toward that maternal life-giver, the Volunteer-labor Association, and the village that gave it birth," Kyung Jae says. "Look, remember, and understand. But, son, remember too, that neither was mother perfect! She too received *some* corruption as a heritage." The older man is feeling somewhat critical as he speaks, "Corruption formed with the initial withdrawal from the ancient Korean relationship with the One God, the Great One, whom we call *'Hananim* [4]!'"

---

3. *Ture/Doorae nongak*

4. The Korean name of the Highest Deity/God of Heaven in primitive and contemporary times.

"Okay, father. I will follow the show, and I will watch the one whose role is the counterpart to mine," Young Kim says, wanting to be as agreeable as possible. "I will watch the leader of the Specialized Farmers Music Group. I will try to learn if this troupe of strolling actors has any form like that which we have obtained as our legacy." "That is fine," his father responds. "Then we will go to visit the village elders to give comfort for those who were injured in yesterday's accident on the road. For they have lost good men, at least temporarily, who also *have orphaned children*, in a manner of speaking. Their families must be grieved."

As Young Kim walks through the crowd, he works his way through the spectators with curious eyes. He looks quickly and as closely as possible at the people in the crowd—everyone he sees—as he encircles the performance area. The crowd, which is a mix of local people, people from the city and from distant places, arouses an unfamiliar excitement in Young Kim. Even the novelty of the crowd causes his heartbeat to quicken. This whole experience is very stimulating. Although the Volunteer-labor Farmers music practices also gather with large groups like this, they consist of ones with whom he lives and works, daily. They are his neighbors, friends and family. Rather than generating excitement, they make the experience of viewing their performance feel natural and relaxed.

As Young Kim collects his thoughts and feelings, a well groomed woman, almost his mother's age, suddenly appears before him from within the crowd. She speaks to him with an air of confidence and boldness. She asks, "Excuse me, are you the son of Kyung Jae?"

Young Kim bows and answers, "Yes, I am. Are you from the city, and who are you; please, can you tell me?" he inquires. "Why are you asking about me?" Curious and surprised, he further questions the woman.

"Oh yes, excuse me." She realizes that she has been speaking her own private thoughts, and is embarrassed that she has actually spoken them aloud. "I have been searching for you in Suwon-san, where I learned that you would be *here*," she explains. "I hope that it will not be inconvenient if we could talk for a short while before the farmers musical performance begins. I have been asked by the parents of Miss Oh to talk with you," the woman further explains. "It has been a long time since we—that is Miss Oh's parents, and I—since we first met."

"Miss Oh! Yes," says Young Kim, now more stimulated. He is very surprised by this unexpected meeting, and does not know how to respond, especially in this unusual environment. Still, he speaks, "Are you uh, uh . . . " he hesitates. "Yes," the woman interrupts. "I am Miss Oh's cousin, Chun Hee."

"Yes, I would have known in a less surprising circumstance.

"Annyong Haseyo!" Young Kim almost shouts, awkwardly and embarrassed, as he bows again to Chun Hee. "I am pleased to see you. It has been such a long time! I was not able to recognize you at first because you look more mature than when I last saw you. Please excuse me . . ." he says, embarrassed again, this time by his error. "It is good to meet you again," he repeats, respectfully. "And do you still work as a marriage arranger?" he asks.

He remembers her from their prior meeting. She returns the greeting, "Annyong Haseyo.[5] Yes. That is why I would like to talk to you, if only for a short time. It is for a professional reason that I would like to talk with you. Please excuse me for meeting you so abruptly, unexpectedly. I will only make an initial inquiry at this time, as I do not want to begin a serious matter without notice, Mr. Paik," Chun Hee says, showing Young Kim respect.

They talk only for a few minutes—and it is difficult to hear clearly, with the great noise, including the shouts and screams of the crowd. Chun Hee does not want to impose—by continuing to talk in such an awkward environment. But, she had come from more than a short distance from Seoul, where she is one of the disappearing numbers of those who work professionally in the field of arranging marriages. Chun Hee spends the next few minutes questioning Young Kim about his relationship with her cousin and about his financial and occupational goals for the future.

She has learned from the parents of Miss Oh that Young Kim is a conservative and traditional-minded farmer. He intends to continue to live in his community which is a redeemed, Christian, Volunteer-labor farming community. Chun Hee also knows that Young Kim's father has done pioneer work with the Volunteer-labor community, working hard with its organization.

After their brief conversation, Chun Hee leaves, returning to Suwon-san to arrange to talk to with her cousin, Miss Oh and her parents about her relationship and the hoped-for marriage with Young Kim.

---

5. The typical Korean greeting, an expression of abundant blessings.

As he shifts his attention to the present moment, Young Kim feels the energy from the people who fill the open area of the marketplace. The musical prelude stimulates them. This is the first time that his father has encouraged him to attend a performance of the Wandering Minstrels. From what Young Kim sees, he feels that their lives are different and more exciting than those of the members of his own Common-labor Association Farmers Music Band. Thus, he muses simply, 'These performers *do* lead different and more exciting lives.'

Now, Young Kim's heart smiles a contented smile. For, even his father is now with him at this opportunity to experience one of the disappearing number of the professional marriage arrangers.

Young Kim watches the tightrope dancers complete their skillful entertainment by jumping high off the rope, and with a twist of the body, to land on the ground. The crowd gasps and cheers in amazement at the spectacular performance happening above their heads. As he continues to walk through the crowd, once again, he, like the others, is captivated. Thus, he does not pay attention to the fact that he has walked away from his father.

Next, he recognizes the familiar sound of a solo lead-singing, and of group-responsive singing—just like the music that he and the band perform during a typical day in the field! He now weaves his way to the place that he feels will give him the best perspective of the presentation. He clearly knows and identifies with the responsive singing which has often given much joy to him and all his co-workers in the fields.

Young Kim cannot count how many times he has led songs in the village fields while those working with him sang responsively, and continued to sing in that mode much of the day.

Young Kim now feels a newfound sense of belonging in this place. He has an abstract, yet real, identification with the *lead singer of the band* [6] He now feels certain that he is in the right place to enjoy the kind of performance, which the people had been talking about for such a long while.

As Young Kim watches, he recognizes a fellow villager from Suwon-san standing next to him. He knows that he is a Volunteer-labor Association member, and exclaims, "Hello! Oh, how polished and excellent this performance looks!" He feels a sense of acceptance to see the lead singer do just what he loves to do! Also, while the group is singing, a clown-play is performed, adding to the enjoyment. The music serves as a narrative to the play. And, scattered around the edges of the audience, expertly-adept plate spinners do bewildering feats of balance, with plates atop long sticks. All around him, the crowd's enjoyment is expressed and demonstrated by loud shouts, excited jumping and arm waving.

"It is difficult to believe that these fellows can play the music that we do—and yet so much more!" exclaims Young Kim to the Suwon-san neighbor. "I am amazed at what I see." He is filled with awe. "They certainly look very talented and professional, to me!" he says, unable to hide the sense of envy in his voice.

At that moment, Ki Jun sees the two young men from Suwon-san standing together, and he approaches them. "Have you ever seen such a talented Farmers Music group? They *are* specialized! With their specialization,

---

6. *Solsori*

they are so refined!" he exclaims, now clearly impressed with what he is seeing.

As the two small boys, nearby, yell loud encouragement to the performers, they begin to hurt their own ears, a little. "Bravo, bravo. How great you are!" they shout. "We would be just like you are. We want to prove to the entire world that we are the best musicians—like you. And we will go anywhere, too, like you"! The boys jump up and down, again and again, continuing to shout and yell out. Then they add, "All the people will love us, like they love you!" When the shouting ends, Young Kim and Ki Jun look at the boys next to them, and recognize them. Young Kim smiles at the boys and say, "You two boys live in this village don't you?"

"Yes, we do," they answer almost in unison. "And we love the Wandering Minstrels."

"We think that it is the best thing in the world to live a life like theirs," says the older brother, Chong Won.

"It is true that they are really so good," Young Kim agrees. With some consideration, he then asks, "Have you boys ever seen a harvest festival or a day of a common-meal at our Volunteer-labor village? You might also think that it is good—and we play too, much like this group of Wandering Minstrels. We do this every day, all the time. Yes, we play and sing at home, where we live!" Young Kim is excited talking to the boys, and he talks not without a little coercion.

Then, Young Kim resumes his conversation with Ki Jun. To answer the question Ki Jun asked before the interruption, he says, "I too, am enjoying this great performance. But, it seems so good that it becomes a distraction, or maybe more accurately—a temptation," he says. Next, the two men notice one of the clown actors making a hand gesture to a man in the crowd, who is standing near Young Kim and Ki Jun. He repeats the gesture, and then begins to laugh, and jumps away, still laughing. At this, Young Kim and Ki Jun look at each other somewhat startled, and with confused and questioning stares. Young Kim wonders if it is like a challenge of an intimate nature, which he has heard was done in circles of professional musicians in historical times. But, then he could not admit that he had really seen it, and thought it might be best to forget it. Meanwhile, Ki Jun silently wonders.

As the performance nears its end, the musicians play a musical finale. Young Kim looks up and begins to focus on his counterpart, the lead singer, who is doing just what Young Kim would be doing in any kind of clown or mask play. He now feels an admiration for the singer which helps bring Young Kim's mind back to the present time. In the same moment, he doesn't recall all that his father has said to him, because of these exciting minutes of the new performance.

Ironically, he can't remember his father's earlier counsel that these musicians' focus would be more upon themselves than their own community, and that they had de-valued the roots of their cultural tradition—and all the rest that his history-burdened father had laboriously instructed his son.

Young Kim begins to feel weary from the high energy-level, the excitement of the performance, the excitement of the crowd, and the length of time standing and bumping against others in the crowd. He is excited, despite that he has begun to feel weary.

He is not accustomed to casually touching people that he's never met—and thinks to himself, 'I don't even touch my friends this much'. So, he begins to feel more tired, despite the heightened level of excitement from his first experience at a Strolling Minstrel performance.

Young Kim is thirsty, so he steps away from the others for a moment. He moves to look for a place that has something refreshing.

Kyung Jae walks through the crowd; he too is being bumped along his path as he walks. Then he sees his son ahead of him, and he continues to walk and walks next to Young Kim. Then, he reaches in the pocket of his jacket and hands a sweet pear and an apple to Young Kim. "Here, Young Kim, eat these. You must be hungry. These are good and sweet."

"Thank you, father. I am a little hungry," he says, now more content. "Let us walk to where the singers and actors are—just over there, Young Kim," Kyung Jae says, pointing the way. Then, he begins to lead the way through the thinning crowd. "There is some time before they begin the next part of the performance. Let's go, and we should be able to meet some of them in the specialized farmers band, son."

As they weave their way through the people—they mix and move about them, the people move from here and there, and everywhere, sometimes into them, sometimes not. The father and son walk nearly halfway across the marketplace when they come upon a few of the performers who have casually put aside their instruments and cast off the outer garments of their costumes. Kyung Jae deeply bows—*first*— despite his age, and sincerely congratulates and thanks the men for their fine performances. Then, he introduces himself and Young Kim, as ones who share some interests with the performers.

Soon, the Wandering Minstrel Group players see that Kyung Jae and Young Kim are farmers, and ask the two men about it—they want to know the meaning of what Kyung Jae had said. The Wandering Minstrels' lead singer, Young Cho, lights a cigarette and grins, and the others mimic the grin. He says, "What is it that you have in common with us, sir? Do you work throughout the country, like we do?" The other performers grin again, as they look quickly at one another's face.

"No, sir," Kyung Jae answers, "our work is focused upon our own village and our nearby neighbor village". "From those places, and without leaving these villages, our joy will reach to the borders of our country. Just as your performances reach throughout the land, Cooperative Labor Farmers Bands can be established in every area of this country. In our village, the people can come from throughout the country to live in one place. We have no restrictions in that sense. Therefore, we are happy to work for the benefit of the entire village. By that I mean eternally!" Kyung Jae adds. Then *he* smiles at the men. "*In our hearts* we, too, are professionals, working with expertise, just as you do."

"Our motivation is from loving our work and loving what is good. Does that interest you?" Kyung Jae adds, "Our *primary motivation* is to love God, *Hananim*—the God of our ancestors.

Having said this, Kyung Jae turns to his son for affirmation. A little startled by his father's candid communication, Young Kim responds with a smile and shakes his head, 'Yes'. Then, the father challenges the men by asking them, "And are you content that you do not demand to know what anybody else would say, or what they would think of you?" Young Kim's smile grows bigger, because he agrees, *and* because he is embarrassed.

Now, a boy approaches the group and hands a small box to one of the performer-band members. The boy is also a member of the troupe; a *child actor*[7] now dressed like a girl. His appearance is according to Asian drama tradition. In the past, child actors have typically been part of both the Specialized Farmers Music Bands and Common-labor Farmers Bands.

The man then takes the box from the boy, opens the top, lest it stand straight upright, and puts the box on the boy's arms. His arms are extended forward from his waist. The man then leans forward and begins to apply makeup from the box to the boy's face, first rapidly glazing lipstick on his lips. Next, he expertly applies a bright pink color. As he continues to apply more makeup, another boy approaches with a woman's dress in his arms. He stands and waits for the man to complete his application of the makeup. But, as the man continues his focused activity, he motions quickly with his hand for the boy to return with the dress to the dressing area, from where he had come.

Another of the troupe's older actors has the appearance of being very experienced, with a well-lined face. He has a glint in his eyes as he looks at Kyung Jae. As he approaches, he stops, bows in Kyung Jae's direction and introduces himself as the leader of the group of Strolling Minstrels. A younger man abruptly says, "He is Jae Kyung, our *organizer*[8] He is our leader, a man of great ability and experience!" At this introduction, Young Kim

7. *Mudong*

8. *Chipsa*—the title of honor for leaders and organizers of groups.

is both impressed and bewildered. Why? He feels that way because the boy's introduction showed such great respect for the leader of the Farmers Band. More importantly, he curiously has a name like his own father's name! The names of the same words in their names—in reverse order! Young Kim continues to wonder about it. 'This is so unusual,' he thinks. 'It is too rare to ignore.'

Jae Kyung, the Wandering Minstrels' leader, then speaks, "Our group of musicians and actors has traveled to many places in this land. We have endured many difficulties. Something more important is that we have endured much of the prejudices which were imposed upon Farmers Music troupes even from the times of the Yi dynasty farmers' riots. Please believe that!" He continues, "Because of those days, and other times, we, who are singing actors, were placed on the same level as prostitutes and the other so-called 'despicable professions'.

"Sir, we love to play our music, to dance, to sing, and act for the people," Jae Kyung recounts. "We work for different reasons. We work to prolong a tradition which was born in this country, and is very old. I have even taken part in the experience of home traditions that have been more or less lost in this country. You, members of a Farmers Band, should know about the noble *"Flower Boys"*[9] They have left us with a heritage that is not well known to many people.

"As Young Kim and his father listen and watch, they both notice a light in Jae Kyung's eyes, brightly shining.

---

9. *Hwarang*—originally formed centuries ago as a group of gifted, knight-like Korean men, they were skilled in the arts, poetry, etc. The group evolved, to later live a renowned lifestyle of traveling and performing.

His voice acquires a depth, reflecting a sense of unique value, as he states, "The noble 'Flower Boys' gave us 'Pretty Boys' also as a heritage." Continuing, he says, "Throughout the years, I have performed in many ways with the knight-like men from historical tradition— those with abundant, diverse abilities and interests." The Wandering Minstrels' leader continues, "I have also performed with the most exciting, farmers music groups."

The role of 'Pretty Boys' is about which the leader of the troupe boasts.

With that word, the visiting men of the Farmers Music Group simply bow, turn, grin to one another, and proceed to make preparations for their next performance sequence.

Young Kim stands silently wondering. He knows what the Farmers Music bandleader meant when he spoke. About that, he could do nothing but wonder in an amazed state of finality. Young Kim turns, looks at his father, and says, "These players are like us, as musicians." Thinking as he speaks, he slowly continues, "We are like them, as ones who perform for the benefit of others." Young Kim pauses. "Yes, we are like them, but we are so very different. I need to consider more deeply what I have seen here, today, father," Young Kim says, still somewhat bewildered and indecisive. After a brief pause, Young Kim's father says, "I am ready to talk to the village elders, now. Shall we begin to walk together?" Young Kim nods his agreement; his father sees his son's answer and says, "Let's go." "Let us take Ki Jun with us," Young Kim adds.

"Mr. Lead Singer, wait for me!" Young Cho calls to his Common labor Association counterpart, as he skip-dances across the open grounds of the now almost empty, deserted marketplace. "I would like to teach you about how to enjoy your life!" The grin, just like that which he had shared earlier with his colleagues, has now returned. But, the tone of his voice somehow betrays a more self-conscious note. Unfortunately, however, due to a distracted mind, Young Kim is not receptive to his counterpart's mood.

"You know that when someone is in a Specialized Farmers Music Group like I am, there are so many opportunities presented," says Young Cho. He continues, now with a noticeable hint of anxiety is in his voice. "But, as a performer in a troupe of wandering actors, I had thought in the first few years, that there would never be anything that would be 'too much for me'. Now, I see problems in my life that even our rites and all good times are not able to make me forget, or overcome! I would tell you that my life with Specialized Farmers music is trouble free. Of course, every person knows about the prejudices—in our history—against professional musicians and singing actors. This problem is not about what others think of me. That doesn't concern me, now. Why? Because I learned at an early age that in a Troupe of Strolling Actors, there are many things available to hide the pains of life—or to cover them, so they are not felt, or realized. Yet, even though we saw much good come from our own prayers; from the *rites* [10] of our style of the Farmers Music and Dance Band, in time, the problems that are now troubling me, began to emerge.

"I do not want to tell you more about my problems, now, as it would not be right to burden you, so abruptly, Young Cho apologizes. "I am amazed how you can live

---

10. *kut*

in a village, without going anywhere to see how the people are in other parts of the land, and that you do not learn of new people and their ways. Those are things we love to do, and that brings excitement to our lives. And, we find fulfillment in those things!"

"Maybe if I had an opportunity like yours when I was small, I too, would be doing what you now are doing," answers Young Kim, with a noticeable hint of jealousy in his words. "Your kind of farmers music—the specialized kind—appears to be something that the people love to watch, and something that you enjoy performing, too!" Young Kim encourages his counterpart. "The lifestyle seems tempting to so many of the people from Suwon-san to whom I have talked," he adds.

"Are you like us when we do our rituals of Farmers Music and Dance with prayers against the evil spirits at the houses in the villages? And, do you pray for one another?"

Young Cho politely asks. He tries not to be perceived as too personal in his anxiety. He also asks if Young Kim visits the shaman.

"To us, the shamanists are like a national treasure." Young Cho now sounds refreshed. The *folk-religionists* [11] —their tradition is like the farmers music tradition, which perpetuates our farmers' folk music," he finishes his thought weakly and unusually enthusiastic.

"The answer to your other question is 'Yes'. We do pray for one another," Young Kim answers. "But, we do not do the ritual according to the traditions of Farmers Music Bands," says the local farmer's young son.

---

11. *mudang*

Young Kim continues, "No, we do not pray against the bad spirits—by asking the favor of the welcoming/guardian spirit, by the big tree at the entrance of the village—as your group does."

Young Kim says, "And, to the last question the answer is 'No'. We do not seek the folk-religionist to take away our pain, nor our problems either." We are not totally like other common-labor, or Volunteer-labor associations that have come before us. We *are* like them before the arrival of the religions of China—Buddhism and Confucianism—and even before our own Korean, folk-religion!"

As he listens, Young Cho stands in silence, almost as if enchanted. Young Kim then continues, "We pray for one another . . . to the *Great One, the God of Heaven* [12.] He was the God of this land *and* the God of the people of this land—before gods were introduced by the religions that followed. No other religion was here, or was needed, until after the Chinese Emperors of the Zhou Dynasty no longer allowed the common people to pay homage to our God, *Hananim* [12], or, as the Chinese called Him, *Shang Di* [12b]. That happened about 3000 years ago.

"For us, He is still *Hananim, The Great One*—as He has always been!" Young Kim says enthusiastically. Now excited, Young Kim feels his ears warming, as they sometimes do when he energetically dances and sings with the band. "As my father has taught me to believe,

12. *Hananim*, is translated, 'The Great One', also understood as 'The God of Heaven'
(12b), 'Supreme God' of ancient, pre-Buddhist, pre-Taoist and pre-Confucian history, and 'The Greatest One; the number One Sir/Lord'. Both the Chinese (11b) and Korean.

each of those who are sorcerers will one day answer to Him whose name is The Great One—like every other human being who will some day do that, too.

"Only He, Hananim, has the right to be God, and not any of us. Not any other!"

Again, Young Kim speaks enthusiastically—he is 'pumped up'. "'The Great One' has nevertheless, sent us someone who is like Him; his Son, who only does the things that He does. He sent us the One that He sent before all the others came; the others that some people in this land now follow. But, we do not follow only the traditions of farmers or folk-religionists who are men and women, only. Yes, we do follow farm traditions, but everything to us can be like the water we drink. It must be clean and healthy, or it is not fit to be taken into a healthy body."

Young Kim now speaks innocently, as a young son— even one somewhat younger than his own age. Thus, he continues, "My father has told me this about prayer in Korea. Let me explain.

"In our village, our model for life began at the beginning of our nation's history," he speaks on, just as his father sometimes does. "Now, we all pray in our Volunteer-labor Association village, just as our ancestors, of ancient times, once prayed. My father and I have learned this; and he says that we should not accept substitutes. We should accept no substitute god."

Young Cho becomes less anxious as he listens, but still not without some anxiety. He says to his new-found friend, "I want to ask you, do you know if the sorcerers and folk-religionists were more effective at overcoming bad spirits with their house-rites or rituals, than your own Farmers Band Music rituals? But now it seems that you do an ancient rite, different than that which most farmers do. It is a reminder of the rituals that the people do in the churches, here. Those rituals are the 'Western learning rituals'." The well-traveled, well-experienced performer explains himself.

"Anyway, would you come with me to the sorcerer, the '*mudang*'?" Young Cho asks his counterpart. "I would like to make an appointment to see if she can cast out from my life, the problems which will not stop. Would you accompany me, lead-singer friend of the Common-labor Association? I would appreciate your companionship so much, along the way. Please, would you come?" he begs.

"Yes. I planned to go that way, already. So, we can go together," Young Kim says, interested in learning more about Young Cho's problem. Then he says, "But, first I must tell my father and friends that I will join them a little later, as it is our plan also to go together, along the East Mountain."

Young Kim then leaves Young Cho and begins to walk in the direction of a cluster of farmhouses where the group is headed. As he walks, he becomes immersed in reflections of all that he has seen and heard that day. Thoughts begin to shoot through his head like bullets. Thus stimulated by his recent experience, he thinks, 'Those Farmer Music Band players are very good musicians—and more! They are skillful in many things. And they travel to so many desirable places. Why should I not be able to use my *talents* in that way, too?' 'The freedom which they have is like none that I really know, nor do the people of our village.'

The performance is such a distraction to Young Kim. He doesn't understand what he has just said about himself and his village—as a follower of the Messiah. His mind continues to run like a racecar at full speed. He keeps thinking about this performer with whom he was walking. 'This lead-singer from the troupe of so-called Wandering Actors is younger than I am, but he has done so much!'

Young Kim's inner dialogue continues on. 'In addition, the heritage of the troupe is of different form than that of the life of a simple, communal-labor farm heritage,' Young Kim senses, as thoughts race through his head.

He walks and thinks so deeply and philosophically that his thoughts become confused. He believes that the opportunity was there for him to expand the horizons of his experience. He thinks that he cannot let this pass him by; since he might never have another opportunity like this.

As he walks along the dry and dusty bank of the rice paddy, he looks up and sees Ki Jun standing alone on the path a short distance ahead, just before the curve on the bank of the rice field. After the curve are the houses where the men will meet for the council meeting of the village leaders and spokesmen, now hidden by the tapering ridge of the mountain, "Hello, our lead musician. How are you, today?" asks Young Kim, as he draws close to Ki Jun.

Amazingly, Ki Jun has been in a similar hyper-state of contemplation of *farmers music and dance* [13] as Young Kim had been, until almost that moment. For that reason, they are able to understand the state of mind of the other;

---

13. *Nongak*

their minds are on the same 'frequency', like two radios, and are therefore able to communicate more easily.

After Ki Jun greets Young Kim, he answers and says, "I asked your father to go ahead without me. After watching that specialized farmers music performance, there are so many new things I have seen! It is so much to me. I feel the need to consider all that I saw. It is not every day that a person is challenged by such a performance as the one that we have seen today."

"Yes. Oh, I was thinking the same thing, now, to myself," says Young Kim. "I cannot stay to talk now, as I said that I would accompany the farmers music group's lead singer, Young Cho, to the house of the shaman, to make an appointment." Will, you please tell my father that I will return soon? Thank you.

"Wait, I'll walk with you some of the way," Ki Jun says. "And, don't they perform their own folk-religion rites in this troupe of wandering actors?"

"Yes," Young Kim answers. "But Young Cho says that he wants to see if the local shaman can give more effective results than their own farmers music band ritual can give. You see, he has told me that their prayers of the rite have not helped his problem. He says he needs help," Young Kim says of his specialized farmers music troupe counterpart. Young Kim feels real concern for Young Cho.

Again, Young Kim's thoughts change and he says, "I am amazed at the number of people that came to this little place to watch the specialized farmers music performers. Even more, I am so impressed with the interaction they had with the people."

"Oh yes!" exclaims Ki Jun. "Here, we have freedom and a joyful time, but the freedom of moving around a crowd of strangers, and expressing yourself so creatively—that idea is so attractive to me! It is very exciting!"

After this brief, but revealing exchange, Ki Jun says, "I must go back now. I will see you soon at the house beyond the curve. Goodbye!"

Suddenly aware, Ki Jun calls, "Mr. Lead-singer[14]," as if awaking from a dream. "But, why are you going to the house of a shaman/folk-religionist, when you have a relationship with the God of Heaven who is greater?" 'He's the greatest, literally,' he thinks to himself.

He does not complete his words, for Young Kim does not respond, since he is too far down the path to have heard. Young Kim is excited, determined, and he now is focused on what is ahead. He will not turn back or be delayed. He walks almost as rapidly as possible, though not too fast, as to appear unrespectable in this village, which is not his own.

Young Kim thinks of what he feels that he has been denying in his heart. He was only slightly able to hear Ki Jun's words as he turned and hurried away to Young Cho and the house of the 'mudang'. He understands the urgent plea called to his back, and he is unable to ignore it.

As he approaches Young Cho, Young Kim wonders, 'What can be done to help this Farmers Music Band performer, whom I must respect? Can I do less than what is effective; what I know to be right and do good?" He thinks this thought as he walks toward Young Cho. 'How will I save face before him? And, how can I hide, in right conscience, at a place where the light does not brightly

14. *Solsori*

shine? *It is* a matter of conscience that I am facing. What a deep challenge this is."

Then, two young boys come from among the houses in the area from which Young Kim has just left. As they run, they pass him on the bank of the rice field. The boys quickly and partially bow, and squeal excitedly about the Farmers Music performance. Young Kim acknowledges them, and smiles at their unintelligible squeals.

"Are you ready to go, my friend?" asks Young Cho with both eagerness and anxiety in his voice.

"Yes, and I want to talk to you as we walk to the house of the shaman. It is only a short distance, and it will not take long to speak of this matter to you," Young Kim explains. He is not really sure what he is about to say, but he wants to be careful not to disturb Young Cho's emotions.

"I have just told our lead small-gong player that I want to go with you, now. And you know, he told me as I left that he thinks it is not good for me to go with you," Young Kim says, uncertainly.

"What reason does he have to tell you that you should not go with me?" Young Cho asks.

"Thank you for asking me," Young Kim answers. He hesitates, and considers the words he is about to speak. "As I have explained to you earlier, the shamans are not the most effective ones to help you overcome problems. This is what we—our lead small-gong player and I— have seen. It is also about what my dear father has seen, and the people of my village know to be true, also. We would not visit shamans," he concludes.

"Because, besides the Farmers Music Band ritual which is a tradition of the strolling performers and the shaman's ritual, I know of no way to get help," Young

Cho insists. He persistently believes that he knows just what Young Kim's answer will be. "But, almost everyone uses the shaman's ritual, Kyung Jae's son," argues Young Cho. "Why would you not want to get their help to remove something that is hurting you? And, who could you go to that can be more effective than the shaman?

But Young Kim says, "Ours is a small village. And, as a Co-operative-labor Association village—and one that follows Hananim—we are a very small minority—both in this region and in the whole country." Young Kim speaks uneasily now, trying to find the right words. "Still, we have been given great success by the One who is there to help us overcome the pain of our hurts and our problems . . ." Then, he hesitates, "Please excuse me, lead singer, for I will not be able to accompany you further, to see the shaman. Please forgive me, I must return, now.

"But," Young Kim adds, "I would feel inadequate if I just left you alone at this point. How may I help you, otherwise?"

"You have truly earned my respect by the way you show interest in me," responds Young Cho. "I appreciate that and for that I appreciate you. It is not often that those who watch our performances show interest in anything other than the excitement of our show and of the life of the 'strolling actor'. On the contrary, you seem to me to be a person of more understanding."

"My problem now seems to be a smaller matter," Young Cho answers.

"It seems smaller since we have had time to talk with one another, and having only musical abilities in common. Now, I will not go to the shaman, either. For I now see that she cannot help me like this 'One' of whom you speak."

Then, Young Kim turns and begins to walk back toward the mountain and the adjacent houses for the village elders' meeting. Young Cho also turns, moves quickly to catch Young Kim, and begins to walk alongside him. Young Cho speaks again, "I would like to have a helper who is better than this shaman, a helper like you have, Young Kim—or, someone even better than our own Farmers Band ritual. It is difficult to believe that there may be a better practice than the ancient folk-religion rite that only *our* nation can call its own.

"Let's talk again, soon, my friend. I think that you are a good man, and a good Volunteer-labor association lead singer. I hope to see you again, very soon. Young Cho's words touch Young Kim's heart—and stimulates him to more deeply consider the young.

CHAPTER IV

ONE MAN TURNS

N ow, suddenly, Young Kim feels more impressed with his musical counterpart as he walks a short distance on the path. He is filled with hope as Young Cho turns off the path, and the two part with a very warm exchange. Young Cho walks towards his fellow performers, who are celebrating and making loud noises. Young Kim's thoughts dance in his head like the dance group in his *Farmers Music* [1] Band. Once again, his

---

1. *Nongak.*

thoughts jump and turn through his mind, at what seems to him a wild pace! He inhales deeply—and then again. Just to take time to stop and breathe deeply seems like an unusual indulgence to him. This mental review helps him to overcome the stress involved with the tension of the day's trials.

The intense thoughts now in his mind are made bearable only by the stimulation, novelty and memories of what he experienced earlier that day. They are also made bearable by the change of heart by his newfound Strolling Minstrel friend. He actually very much enjoys the process by which his mind reviews the day, and his responses to it, as it is less stressful than previously.

As he walks along the impacted sandy brown texture of the rice paddy's bank, Young Kim is surprised when he looks up to see Ki Jun coming toward him on the path. Ki Jun is fairly close before Young Kim sees him. A little startled, Young Kim exclaims, "Oh! I did not expect to see you coming *this* way on the bank—especially not *you*!

Haven't you been involved in the meeting of . . ." Young Kim stops and doesn't finish his thought.

"Please forgive the interruption. The men wanted me to come this way and be sure that you are not having any problems," Ki Jun tells his *lead singer* [2]. I am glad you are here. It would be good to talk a short while as we walk back. Is it all right with you to do that? "

"Yes, that would be good, as we need to talk more," responds Young Kim. "Let us begin. I have some ideas I would to like share with you. Our new friend, one from

---

2. *Solsori.*

the *Group of Strolling Minstrels*[3] was having some difficulty. But, I am greatly encouraged that he has decided to wait to find a better answer for his problem.

"His problem does not seem to be a bad one, to me. There cannot be too much to worry about when he knows that he will leave this place after another performance. Then, he will not have to look at the same place day-after-day, like some people have to do," Young Kim muses.

"Mr. Lead-singer," Ki Jun says respectfully, "we have learned and seen much of specialized farmers music today, through this troupe of strolling actors." Ki Jun speaks now in a cautious manner. "I am surprised that I have not seen much difference between our *Common-labor Association Farmers Music and Dance*[4] and the music and dance of this troupe of Strolling Actors!

"You know, Young Kim, their style of living seems to have strong merits. From my point of view they are worthy of respect as musicians, and as performers. They help each other and work together well." Having said that, Ki Jun pauses. Then, he asks, "What do you think?"

"I think I must consider that question more before I can answer," replies Young Kim. "But, we must not make any quick judgments. Yet, how can you or I ignore such an obvious opening to an occupation which is so much suited to our abilities? Do you think that the value of Farmers Music and Dance, being so practical, is what has drawn so many talented individuals—for centuries? And, because *that* may be true, shouldn't we investigate what this broadened world of Farmers Music can offer

---

3. *Namsadang p'ae.*

4. 4. *Ture/Doorae Nongak, Common labor* Farmer music and dance

us? I think we should look at its benefits. Do you agree, Ki Jun?"

"Yes, Mr. Lead singer, we should not let a rare opportunity pass us by."

"Yes, could it be an advantage to make the move from a passive, static life of doing daily farm work, with music, to the active lifestyle of Specialized Farmers' Music and Dance?" asks Ki Jun, as he stops to remove a small stone which had lodged in his shoe. Ki Jun bends down slightly, as his friend watches him search for the obstruction. Then, he looks up and out to regard the growth in the nearby field of the soon to be harvested rice.

Instead, he responds, "Let us see if there would be a place in this Specialized Farmers Music Band. Perhaps they would be willing to expand, if they see how we can help the performances." Now, Ki Jun lets a novelty of life excite him.

"We could learn other skills, too. Perhaps one of us could dance on the high tightrope, and the other might learn to spin saucers. I am sure you would excel, because you have very quick hands, Ki Jun.

"Yes, and I could even improve my singing abilities," Young Kim says, already imagining himself performing in the other group. Continuing his dream, he says, "Would you love to roam among the crowds and show them your talent? We would also collect the money! I have never done anything like that—or even thought of it! It might be a fulfilling thing to collect a great amount of money after singing difficult songs and, in a new place . . . Can you imagine?"

"Oh!" Ki Jun exclaims. "Then," he says, jokingly, "the rest of the band would have to find new jobs. The people would be interested only in your performance, and not ours! Ha ha!" Ki Jun laughs, and smiles at his fellow musician and watches as he pulls a small, sharp stone from his slip-on shoe.

He tosses the stone far into the rice field. "Now we can proceed to the meeting, without further delay," Young Kim says. The young band leader now focuses his interest on the meeting, which he believes will affect the workload of the whole village.

"Our plans for the future may change. I haven't even thought about what we would be leaving behind, if we go. But, what a change it would be!" he exclaims, still fired by the excitement of the day.

CHAPTER V

EVALUATIONS

N ow, the two young farmer-musicians approach the place where the bank of the rice paddy curves to their left and winds around the sloping heel of the mountain. As they walk, they share the refreshing scent of the pines growing above and they near an area of trees that grow down the mountain, giving the mountainside a hidden and wild look. That seems especially to contrast to the evenness of the rice fields. Both men feel excited as they imagine and anticipate the possibility of a dynamic change in lifestyle.

Filled with expectations, they begin to recount them to one another, and their response to all they have seen that day. They converse as they look back along the path to the place they had encountered one another only a short while earlier. Only this time, to the surprise of both young men, Miss Oh appears unexpectedly in their sight.

Miss Oh is dressed plainly, yet attractively, and as always, seems to be filled with peace. She keeps her clothes clean and attractive at all times. Still, she is also careful not to give an appearance of seduction or allure. Young Kim sees the modesty of Miss Oh as an added bonus to her attractiveness. Traditional values are important to Miss Oh. She feels confident with the values that her farm-village heritage have handed her, and she knows she shows considerable respect for her parents as she maintains those values. She also sees, through years of experience, that in times of avoidable friction in family matters, her positive responses bring harmony — not frustration, which more and more frequently is being experienced by other Korean families. She is thankful for this relatively 'frictionless' life.

Generally, unity follows when she practices the rural traditions peculiar to her own family. She feels a strong, shared bond of loving respect for family tradition with Young Kim. Thus, her joy of seeing her hoped-for fiancé, by surprise, is not well hidden.

Ki Jun quickly anticipates the situation and feels awkward. Spontaneously, he decides to attend the elders' meeting as a non-elder participant and communicates his need to leave, at the appropriate time.

"Hello Miss Oh!" Young Kim says affectionately, and expresses it by bowing deeply in response to her bow. He intentionally uses a lighthearted inflection in his voice when he first greets her. He then plans to develop the friendship in an increasingly friendly manner, without being too forward or personal. His also intends to demonstrate his care for her in a creative way.

She responds in a soft, sweet voice, "It is nice to see you."

Young Kim is honored, and feels a strong attraction. After savoring her presence, he says, "Did you see the performance today at the marketplace?" She carefully greets him again, and answers, "Hi, Young Kim. It is nice to see you. Yes. But I only saw the last part of the performance. I watched for less than an hour because I wanted to come this way for the women's meeting. They are cooking together for a common meal tonight. I heard only their singing, and saw some drama of the performance."

"Miss Oh, that performance made my eyes dance!" Young Kim speaks enthusiastically, using a metaphor, his favorite mode. He speaks in a melodic tone, hoping to make the lightness of his voice match his words, not to sound too 'heavy'. "And the performance has given me inspiration and makes me feel that there is much more to life than to live and work with the same people, day after day. Can you think of, or imagine the possibilities for someone like me, who is able to perform many of the same things that these specialist Farmers Music performers do? Freedom, and liberty . . . which are so refreshing—so . . . uh, new," he quickly edits himself. *That* excites me."

Miss Oh responds with silence, and stares impassively at her soon-to-be fiancé. Her face mirrors both a question and a cloud of uncertainty, which remain in her eyes. She silences and covers a cry. A word, caught back, comes out only as a low sound in her throat. Now, she is embarrassed. Her face remains motionless, and she cannot feel if her heart still beats in her chest. She scarcely breathes.

Unaware, and with unrestrained excitement, Young Kim continues, "Now, to be truly responsible, there are some new things to consider." He now sounds like a businessman to Miss Oh. She cannot remember him ever before speaking in this manner. It seems like she's listening to an intellectual. Still, he adds, "For example, for the first time in my life, I will be able to earn enough money to buy new instruments, as often as I would need them—just as those performers that we both saw today, are able to do!" Young Kim enthuses himself. "I will also be free to play new songs and to develop my skills, as never before. How could I have lived so long and not found an opportunity like this? How can I let it pass me by?" Young Kim is barely hiding the childlikeness, or childishness, of his excitement.

Miss Oh only swallows, with difficulty and some discomfort, as Young Kim continues to talk.

"It is like the times of the Yi Dynasty. It is as if we have been living life in an isolated place. And, to me it is like we are without a way to overcome the government oppression of farmers—just as the way it once was!" Young Kim verbalizes his imagined fantasy, not fully aware of the picture or symbols his words actually paint. As he allows himself to feel a feeling almost like one of being oppressed, he says, "Now, there is a possibility to rise up from the midst of a limited life in a remote place and enjoy the honor of living with a higher potential. There is a chance to live among others who also can determine what their future will be." Stunned, Miss Oh clearly does not understand the basis of his reasoning.

"I could play music, travel, and be the master of my destiny. Then, my life would not be subject to every inherited idea of what is right and good. My family and the others . . ." Young Kim paused, feeling drunk with the excitement of his mind-journey.

Then, as suddenly and unexpectedly as it overcame him, Yong Kim begins to realize the selfishness and awkward state of his mind. His mind was completely void of thoughts of the promise of a long, fulfilling life with the young woman with whom he was talking. Despite an inward sense of shame, he stiffly says, "And you. Perhaps someday all of the village might also discover the opportunity to become more creative. Or, you could even become sensitive enough to respond to life's voice. It will be calling your name in the wind.

"You cannot run away from that kind of call forever, Miss Oh!"

Miss Oh is shocked and cannot believe what she is hearing. Again, she is unable to respond. She numbly struggles to gain perception of the meaning of Young Kim's words. She can only understand that he talked as a person bewitched by something. She looks at the face of a stranger before her and thinks, 'Certainly, he is charmed by the new and different farmers band performance.' She can only relate by reflecting on her own youthful experience of some significant, novel excitement, which, in hindsight, she knows was childish excitability.

Within herself, Miss Oh groans with numb pain. And she does not speak. The expression that finds its way to her face is a weak smile, showing the lostness of her feelings. She comforts herself slowly as she watches this man whom she loves, and as he talks of this 'new dream'. Nevertheless, Young Kim continues to vocalize his imaginations.

In a desperate effort to gain understanding, Miss Oh reasons to herself, 'What he is saying is like symbols of words,' as she remembers his affection for metaphors. She sees this as a symbol of two puzzles. The first enigma is that he is like somebody rising up from among the *Common people* [1]. But, now, he is now joining the ranks of the *Noble elite*. [2] It is like a 'rags to riches story'. As a nobleman, he could now acquire all the privileges and honor of the highest 'rank' of Korean people. The other symbol he seems to speak of, is the division of our own countrymen. It is a symbol of brother divided against brother, and sister divided against sister!

Now, it is Miss Oh's mind that races. She thinks, processing, and knowing how vital and critical this matter is. 'Oh, Young Kim is speaking symbolically about our beloved country. It has been split right in half by foreign military leaders. Others too, of our fellow countrymen who teach men to kill their own brothers—just to fulfill an ideal! It is an unproved philosophy, without distinction. It is like a symbol of the Communist, totalitarian-separatist, in Korea.' 'What more powerful symbol can there be? The tragic division of the tribal-culture of Korea, with already thousands of years on this penin-

---

1. *Minjung*
2. Yangban

sula,' is the answer. As a result, whole clans and entire families are split. And, with a leader who speaks of reunification—even at the cost of more lives. These symbols are too much,' Miss Oh concludes. She feels totally overwhelmed. She is numb.

'But, how is that possible?' Miss Oh, still reasons in her mind, as she stares blankly at Young Kim. To her amazement, he returns the stare! Then, each potential spouse glances away and back again. She continues her thought, 'Why is this possible *only* when a man follows an ideal which is important enough? Then, he will be separated from his family, his closest friends and all that he has known and loved.'

Miss Oh is as amazed with her own grandiose thoughts, as she is with the newly-idealized imagination of Young Kim. As she completes her own thoughts, her mind still seems trapped, as in a fog. The fog is from the anesthetic of disbelief. Through that fog she scarcely hears Young Kim say that they are late for the meeting. Still, she remains transfixed and watches as he leaves, even as if she is actually dreaming. Ki Jun stands and watches in silence the entire time. He leaves with Young Kim.

Miss Oh stands alone on the rice paddy's bank, and cries out to God.

The day's beauty remains visible as the sun rests on the top of the mountain, and then slowly drops behind it. To Miss Oh, it is an eternal moment, painfully isolated from all reality. In one sense, she feels isolated; although, she sees that in His presence, the feeling of the unexpected harshness of human nature's surreal and bitter-numb reality will end in victory.

Then, she thinks, although with pain, 'How can I depend upon anyone?' Her thought moves forth, and away from the present circumstance. Uninterrupted, her thoughts all flee to the place that she can only hope for. Her ultimate hope is beyond her own present and momentary strength to the limitless strength and power of the Transcendent One.

CHAPTER VI

TWO AGAINST ONE

D an Bae speaks of the chill of the early night as she and her husband approach their empty house. She volunteers to go to the kitchen angle-area of the traditional, Korean, 'L'-shaped house, to build a fire that will provide welcome heat. At that moment, they both very much appreciate the ancient, Korean invention of *the sub-floor, centralized heating system.*[1]

She remembers when she was a girl helping her mother cook at the 'turn in the 'L" on cool and cold nights. She remembers how she learned that the location of the outside cooking area was centralized and prac-

---

1. *ondol.*

tical. Now, she enjoys the economy to be able to cook and heat the house, at one time! Dan Bae secretly is still amazed at this dynamic invention; she is so amazed, that she even began years ago to enjoy making the fire to heat the rooms for the cold nights.

To offset the evening chill, Kyung Jae looks forward to drinking a hot cup of tea with his wife. Kyung Jae offers to get the tea, and says, "Dan Bae, I will also prepare some honey from the container, for the tea."

She answers, "The water will be hot, very soon!" They enjoy *ginseng tea*[2] together, as a traditional favorite and a good discipline for health.

'This has been a special day for us.' Kyung Jae thinks as he recalls the actual experience of the Specialized Farmers Band performance.

He then begins to remember so many things that for a very long time he had neglected. He feels a vague 'calling from within', but he cannot easily identify it.

Soon, he has an unexpected realization. Since he has seen the traveling minstrels, he is now better prepared to help his son to understand what they have seen. He will tell Young Kim more about the beginnings of the Volunteer-labor Farmers music and dance, as well as more of the specialized farmers music and dance. He knows that he can offer a better understanding of how the two are similar, and more importantly, how he sees them as essentially different.

'Yes . . . Young Kim will benefit from that knowledge,' Kyung Jae thinks to himself. 'I know that I love to tell of the depths of our cultural heritage, which is so rich and honorable. I will answer and tell him about what he

---

2. *insam cha*

has asked me, before. I will tell this in a 'profound way'. My words will have more power than to just give another historical account to my son.

'I believe that he will enjoy this,' Kyung Jae continues his thoughts. 'I hope he does enjoy it. I know that like most Koreans, he knows the *Tan-gun* creation story. Since it is the important account of the beginning of history, which begins in Korea, I will first use that story as a refresher to re-open his memory. Then, I will use it to show him how we can see that story of Korean origin as a landmark—the story that we have been given.'

"Do you think that the national origin story can be seen as an historical landmark, Dan Bae?" he asks his wife.

Dan Bae quickly agrees that it can.

"First, I can use the creation story to portray the ancestral lifestyle of thousands of years ago, and how we live now," he speaks aloud what he had been silently thinking. "The creation-story landmark can be a landmark, and a model, too. It is not a symbol that can represent the lifestyle of any special, cultural group that does not improve Korea's growth, or the growth of the world."

Meanwhile, the villagers all walk back along the road to Suwon-san, as Young Kim's parents remember their own first days of meeting and engagement. At the same time, Young Kim has a strong desire to return to the camp of the band of strolling actors to see the performer, Young Cho, whom he met earlier in the day. He is interested in their shared abilities, and to learn more of this performer's work-lifestyle.

He will try to learn as much as possible, in as little time as possible. He also wants to hear some of his father's thoughts, before he prepares for sleep.

Young Cho happily greets Young Kim as he approaches the camp. "I saw you coming from the direction where we had walked together, earlier. I have just finished our mask dance, so please excuse my costume. Can we talk for a little while?"

Young Kim agrees, "Certainly, that is fine, but I can only talk for a short while, because the rest of the village has returned to Suwon-san and I must talk to my father about today's events. Yes, I would enjoy very much to talk for awhile. And, you know," Young Kim begins, "it would be a great challenge to me to live like you do. You do the mask dance, the *village rite*[3] at the 'spirit tree' at the houses, and other folk-religion activities. But, we never do that because we have been taught that it is not right according to our heritage. It is not pleasing to God. According to how I was raised, I should not even watch those rites."

"It is interesting that you would say that," his counterpart replies. "For only moments before you arrived, I began to consider if there is not a better way than to rely upon these practices of our ancestors, or to rely on our professional predecessors—even though I have done this for a long time. And I have always thought that this tradition is good. And, I like to think that it is the patriotic and Korean thing to do, even as life in this Specialized Farmers Music and Dance Band is a creative and patriotic way to live.

"I love the freedom and enjoyment that this life offers me," Young Cho adds. "Still, I feel that there is something more. I feel that there is a stronger power available

3. *mudang kut*

105

to me—a power that will give me more contentment than what we have," he says.

Eager to respond, Young Kim says, "What I have seen here, Young Cho, is a man who is working hard, and is committed to that work, and who lives a life which looks to be filled with excitement every day!" Young Kim is enthused. "That man is you! Oh, and the mask dance that you do! It is a significant part of the history of the *Common people*,[4] of the not-so-recent past. It seems to portray a people limited to a minor mode of expression in a repressive and unjust social system. These mask dances were the real voices of the common people," Young Kim continues. "The voices of masses of those oppressed or abused commoners were crying and shouting out, in times past when they did not have rights or a voice like the aristocratic noblemen who ruled the land under the king."

"That is true, Young Kim. Yes," answers the talented performer. And he adds, "Sometimes I ask myself, 'Why do I do Buddhist dances and rituals and *folk-religion rituals* [5] one day, and the next day I do a satire drama about decadent Buddhist monks from history?' But, they did not do the dramas day after day, like I do them now. It was not the intention to perform those dramas as a vocation."

Each man is unusually open to the other. Still, they are also both very curious and a little cautious.

Young Cho continues to express the depths of his heart to this man whom he personally knows—almost

---

4. *Minjung*

5. *Mudang kut*, same as 'village rituals', performed at the village tree. See #3, above.

not at all. "I feel that it is another way to entertain the people, and I enjoy doing these performances. Now, I feel like asking a question. Is my thinking just useless? Maybe it is just useless worry!" he says, confirming his own doubts.

Young Kim has a desire to encourage, and he does not want to criticize. So, he answers, "Your gift is great, Young Cho. Do not think that it is a small thing. My abilities, which are not as varied or great as yours, are worth enough that it helps me to lead the village farmers to do more productive work on the farm. For that, I am very thankful. For in that way, I am just as my parents also have taught me to be. My parents are my example. So, why should you worry when your abilities are greater than mine? I would now love to be able to perform as you have. Your life appears to be really so exciting, Young Cho," Young Kim says, as he expresses a newfound jealousy. Ironically, these words of Young Kim come as a big surprise to Young Cho.

"Oh! It is getting late," Young Kim says, and sucks up a little air as he figures the time he needs to go to his parent's place. "I must go. Thank you for the privilege of permitting me to see your great performance, today!" Then, he turns and makes his way into the dark of the night. He walks quickly along the path, anticipating his father's answers which he hopes will soon be very important to him. And, they will be important *very* soon!

CHAPTER VII

NOT OUR WILL,
BUT YOURS

"I'll see you tomorrow," says Young Cho, half declaring and half questioning. He has not yet told Young Kim what is truly troubling him deep within. He is becoming more ill-at-ease with his part in the troupe. He is troubled by the Strolling Actors' supplications in the *Farmers Music rites*. The village exorcist rituals also performed by his band—are sources of real discomfort. He thinks the things that Young Kim has told him seem simpler. He is becoming dissatisfied and burdened with the rituals: making supplication to so many gods—to bless, to pay for, and for so-called 'peace'. 'This is not real peace,' he thinks to himself. Though he feels better since he talked to Young Kim, he does not feel peace in his mind, or in his heart.

Young Kim walks home, quickly. As he enters the house, his parents are still sipping their hot tea with honey. By now, the house is warm and his parents have made themselves comfortable. Young Kim's mother wants to share that comfort with her son, and offers, "Young Kim, would you like some *tea*? [1] There is some water that is heated, so we all can enjoy some tea together, after your day of excitement." With those words she stands and turns to get his tea. Soon, she returns carrying her favorite tray. It is a beautiful classic, Korean, black-lacquered tray, inset with mother-of-pearl. This lovely tray is one like those found in many Korean homes along with other lacquered furnishings. The gleam and luster of the tray reflects her smile, which shines; for she enjoys times like this very much, to be together only with her family. As she places the cups on the low table, Young Kim thanks her, and then his father begins to speak the things in his heart and on his mind, especially of his son.

"Young Kim, didn't we see some things today that looked very attractive and glamorous? I would like to tell you about what I saw, that you may already know."

"I'd like you to be able to understand better what we have both seen. You will hear something about which you already have some knowledge. I want to show you how you can actively use that knowledge. It will become more than just stored information in your mind. The people have such a great supply of information in their

---

1. *cha.*

minds. It is always good when we use that knowledge more often."

Young Kim remains silent. He thinks that he might already know what his father is going to say. He feels within that he does not want to hear any negative thing, in any form, about today's performance. He will honor his father's request, however, and respectfully listen.

"I think you know what I will say. Yes. I am going to recount the creation history of our land. Some call it the creation myth of Korea, because the story is very old, and has passed from generation to generation for centuries. That is not a problem. We shall see if the truth that we have will cast any light upon the story and what we have all seen today."

"In the beginning . . . there were no people living in our land," Kyung Jae begins. He speaks slowly and intentionally. "In heaven was God the grandfather, according to the 'Kogum Book' which tells of Korea's ancient history. The grandfather's name is Hwan-in. Do you remember that name, Young Kim?" his father asks, as his desire is to maintain a close account in the conversation.

"Yes, father, of course I remember the names of the Tangun story."

"Good," Kyung Jae responds. "Then there is Hwan-woong, the spirit, the father of Tangun. The son of Hwan-woong is Tangun, the god man. You do remember all those names?" he asks to confirm. Young Kim nods his assent.

"According to our ancient creation myth, Tangun asks Hwan-woong's permission to come to earth and to teach the people how to live the right way. Then he came and became the father of Korea, to which he gave the

110

name *Chosun*[2]!" the father speaks excitedly about this ancient mythical-historical account. "That name is one our ancestors have used for centuries. Because he gave the simple people lessons in right living," Kyung Jae says as he moves closer to the hotter area of the floor, nearer the *ondol*.

"Thus, Korea had its first ruler—a great one. It has been attributed to him as the guide and inspiration of all great things that our country has ever received." Kyung Jae stresses this point. Then, Kyung Jae stops speaking, and looks into the eyes of his son with fatherly compassion, especially because he is feeling 'patriotically nostalgic'. To this point, both men are at peace with their time together.

Then, filled with emotion, Kyung Jae swallows and continues to communicate—silently— the importance of the moment to his son. He does so by conveying his sense of love, and by waiting for just the right moment to communicate his thought. He wants to be able to paint the word picture he holds in his heart.

"Please listen closely now, son," Kyung Jae suggests and remains totally still. His son listens intently, and also becomes very still. "There is a story that is like the story I just told. There are two accounts that have many things in common. So, you may easily understand this, as many others do, who might think of, and understand the clear connection.

"The second story is the fulfillment of the Tangun story—the story that I have just told you about. This other story is special and rare because, like the first, it also involves this land." The room now becomes com-

---

2. *(Land of the) Morning Calm*

111

pletely silent. Kyung Jae hesitates, then again continues to speak. "Less than one-hundred years ago—like only a breath since the beginning of Korean history—we were entrusted with the good news of the second story," Kyung Jae says. He now speaks slowly with the desire to be clearly understood by Young Kim. "The second story is not a myth, but it is true."

It is brought forth from the most well-documented history of all time! This historical truth has become a challenge for so many of our countrymen. And, it is a problem for us and much of the whole world." Kyung Jae waits, so that his son can savor the value of the words he has just shared with him.

"In this real story there are also three divine Ones, like the first story. In this real story, there is no grandfather. There is a Father. This *Father* is the Father of everybody, and of everything! He is the *Father of everything that lives*."[3]

Kyung Jae thinks that his parallel is beginning to be stretched. "Nevertheless," he continues, "there is the Godman who is the Son, just as in our ancient, creation myth.

"Also, Young Kim, with the *Real, True* Father and Son, there is a Spirit, which also is God. The Spirit is *the Spirit of the Father*, and He is co-equal with the Godman-Son and the Father. In this real story, the three are One! This Father is the *One* God; He is the equivalent of the grandfather of our creation-myth, Hwan-in."

"I will say it again; in this second, true account there is no grandfather, but a Father, *the Father*. This is important," Kyung Jae says to his son. "This One Father, like

---

3. *Hananim aboji*

the grandfather-god Hwan-in, has a plan for His Son—and, He has, a plan for the whole earth, and for everyone and everything in it!

"But, there is a technical problem, Young Kim. Many know that the Divine Man, the Son, lived on earth a long time ago. But, it was a time that was about a third to half of the total time since the time Tangun is said to have come to earth here in Korea. Tangun is said to have come down 6,000 years ago, either more or less. They see the Tangun myth as a taste of—and a clue to—the real story which was to follow. Others accept the Tangun creation story as the real, ancient, and historical endowment to Korea.

"Now, here is what brings the second story to this room, tonight . . ." Kyung Jae continues to speak. He speaks slowly and clearly, with anticipation. "It is because more and more people want only the real story. The real story *only*—without a copy. They say that the 'taste' or 'clue' which others have, as I mentioned, is a trick, or a way of deception. So, they say that the second story, that is true, will not be believed by the people, if there are two, so very similar, stories.

"Consider with me, Young Kim. People ask, 'Why should there be two stories that are so similar? We have our own heritage, which includes the Korean creation story. So, why do we need another like it, from some *other* land?' That is a good and important question."

With this, Kyung Jae looks into his son's eyes and says, "Young Kim, you must know that the second story is real. It is true! It can never be truly re-created, never! The Godman Son, who is the *Word of God,* cannot ever be *truly* re-created. This is difficult, because some think that it seems to discredit the Korean creation story, and even our culture!"

"But, there cannot be another story like the real one. Please listen and understand this, son. *The people of Korea prayed to the Great One, very long before there was any other god or supernatural power known in this land.* The Great One is the very Father of everything. He is the Father. And, the grandfather in the Tangun creation myth was made to have a position like Him.

"And, more than one hundred years ago," Kyung Jae begins, and repeats. "More than one hundred years ago— it was only then did we learn that this 'Father of everything' sent the Divine Man, whom we call the *Messiah* or *Christ*, to earth to show the people what He is like. He sent His Son to live a perfect life—the life of God-on-earth. They called Him Immanuel, meaning *God is with us.* He came to teach the people by His example, the right way to live. Again, our Tangun myth is just like that."

"But father, many of the people know there are some people that say man cannot be taught how to live. Some say that one needs to experience life—and to learn the best way to live. Recently, I have heard it said that to truly enjoy life, the people have to learn by the wisdom of their own knowledge."

"Young Kim," his father begins, and then pauses to correctly order his words. "There is only one way that man can be taught how to live, *now*. The Son left the Spirit of God here on earth. The Spirit of God comes to live in our hearts when a person is spiritually reborn. The Spirit of God is here to teach all who receive the real, true Son, all about the Son. This is what we know as being *reborn*. The Son has been proved to be the real

Son by the millions who accept Him, and are radically changed to be like Him. And, they are taught how to live by the Spirit of God and the Word of God. That way, they, and we, are able to experience knowing the Father, especially through the knowledge of the Son. For that, you and I, your mother, and so many in Suwon-san, and everywhere, constantly give thanks to the Father, *Hananim!*" Kyung Jae happily exclaims.

"You already know that He did not come directly to Korea to live, but . . . " Kyung Jae again becomes careful, and waits, as he focuses on this fact, which could cause many Koreans to be intellectually or spiritually challenged.

"You are talking about Jesus of Nazareth, who is the *true* Divine Man, correct, father?" Young Kim asks the question to confirm his father's thought.

"Yes, Young Kim, of course," his father answers encouragingly. "He was sent from heaven to a faraway land, far from here, in the Middle East. He was sent to Israel. And, His home, Nazareth, is in Israel. Almost two thousand years since then, the reality of the second story I am telling you, arrived here in our land. Yes, He arrived here in our homeland, in the same land of the Tangun creation story."

Kyung Jae adds, "In that land, Israel, they had written for hundreds of years that the Godman, Jesus Christ would come to earth. After He died and was resurrected, his life of teaching the way of love was brought here to live in the hearts of His people. French and American missionaries brought news of the Godman, the Christ, to us. And, they brought Him to us, by His inspired Word."

"Is there still the same problem, father?" Young Kim asks about the creation stories, while he thinks that he knows the answer.

"The problem is not that the people believe the *real* story—either with or without a copy," Kyung Jae says with the voice of authority. "The problem is that there are so many people who *do not* believe the *real* story. This may seem difficult to realize Young Kim, but our *Hananim* the God of Heaven, 'the Father', sent the God-Man, Jesus, to us. We know that is real. We know He is real, and we know it is true.

Many, many people wrote about the Him when He was on earth. Some were religious who wrote. Many of those wrote what the Father inspired them to write. Others, who had no spiritual connection to the Father, or the Son, wrote some of exact things that the inspired writers had written. *How does that happen*, Young Kim?" the father emphatically questions, while smiling within.

"The God-Man showed us who God the Father is. Before He came as the God-Man, He lived forever in heaven, with the Father and the Spirit, and He then, forty days after He was resurrected, He returned there. And now, there He lives, and there He will be forever, also! Except, that is, when He comes back to earth to claim His bride, His people."

"Now, the Godman, Jesus Christ, has given us the responsibility to tell and show others how to live, just as He has shown us." Thus Kyung Jae explains, simply, the gospel and great commission. "As we submit to His supernatural life and power, He comes to live in our hearts through the Holy Spirit. Then, as we are guided and empowered by the Holy Spirit, we can accomplish that assignment. We become like Christ through the

Spirit of the Father living in us. All this is not limited to our country, only. It involves the whole world. That is why I say that we truly need the true story. Not because it involves only our beautiful country. It also involves the entire world.

"For that purpose, the Divine Man came and went from the earth, a special Gift. Then, He left another Gift—the Holy Spirit—to tell us everything about Jesus and to help us show others how to live the good, abundant life," Kyung Jae says, keeping the emphasis on the godly aspect.

"Here again, we see the example to show us how to live is in the creation myth and in the real story. The gift He brought here to us in Suwon-san is how to live—and how to live a committed, co-operative-labor lifestyle. We are to follow the example of the God-Man's life on earth. The co-operative-labor association's lifestyle is one that allows us to help others; to live to serve each other for the good of all and for God's sake. And, importantly, the lifestyle is voluntary, chosen—and never forced. Young Kim, do you have any questions about this?"

"Does that mean, father, that many people with Western learning must come here, and go to the countries around us to tell of the Gift? And, will they still come to tell us of what we have already learned?"

"Those are good questions, and difficult ones, Young Kim," Kyung Jae answers his son. "If the people would live exactly the way that the Spirit of God has taught them to live, maybe there would not be a need for people to travel long distances to share the knowledge and life they are learning from God's Spirit.

"Can you see in the villages around our village how many people want to be the most important person? So many want to be more important than the Greatest One, *Hananim*. "It is for that reason that the Son directed us to go into the entire world to share His good news with them, the news to surrender one's life and to live forever in heaven with God. But, so many have not heard that news. So many others are confused or just do not want to give up loving themselves and their own way of life. Others will not submit themselves—to anyone!

"How can we live our *Cooperative Farmers Band*[4] life here in Suwon-san, and go to the entire world? Can we stay and go? That seems very difficult, father. It really seems impossible!" Young Kim speaks boldly, hoping to present a challenging response to his father's wise sayings. "Aren't we sharing the good news well enough here, by living, loving even the poor ones, and working hard at what we do, father?"

"You ask more excellent questions, Young Kim. Certainly, you know now, that God speaks to each person, and tells him and her in their hearts. He gives some a strong desire to go. Some, He does not. Or, God will give specific answers to those who ask Him what He wills them to do for their service in their village, or outside of the village or city. You know how we have been given a strong and clear interest and compassion for the people of the next village. This, I think, is unusual, Young Kim. Maybe there are many villages that get to help the next village, but much more often Hananim will speak to a person's heart, as an individual. He speaks in response to the heart-cry of each of those who live according to His Spirit.

---

4. *Ture/Doorae nongak*

"If others live by helping one another—even to a small degree, by giving of their time, and moreover, one's physical resources, they too can find the precious gift. And, importantly, the lifestyle is voluntary, chosen—and *never* forced. It is lived to constantly bring honor only one Person."

"That one Person is the most important part of our life. We can live the way we live only while we acknowledge from Whom, and from where the gift to us has come," the farmer-father says, teaching his son. "We must always acknowledge the true source of every good capability that we have. Farmers music and dance of *Volunteer-labor associations*[5] is a rare and precious thing. It is an invaluable gift, to be ever appreciated while never forgetting the Divine source, Young Kim."

Kyung Jae is careful to speak specifically and thoroughly to his son about these extremely important things. So, he continues, "Only with the practice of constant appreciation can the gift be kept from being corrupted. The God of heaven gave us the ability to develop the tool of Farmers music and dance.

"He must be given all credit for everything that He has given. We must always thank God. If we do not give Him the credit that is due to Him, then the tool can be corrupted. And, the Creator, the provider of the tool, wants to see the loving thanks that He places in the hearts of His people through the God-Man, Jesus, by the Spirit of God.

"You see, Young Kim, the Father is displeased when the tools He gives are rejected or misused. To reject the tool is in some way like rejecting the Father!

---

5. *Ture/Doorae*

"To copy *the story* may be like copying the *Volunteer-labor association Farmers music and dance*[6]," Kyung Jae says. He speaks no more. He is himself surprised at the peace he finds through speaking these words to his son. The wind then lightly vibrates the wooden panel of the door.

Dan Bae smiles at her husband. She is content to listen, because she holds virtually the same spiritual beliefs in her heart as her husband. And, as much as possible, the couple works hard to be in accord, especially for their son's sake. The house's warmth and comfort motivate her to rise and take the hand of her husband, excuse herself, and lead him to the ondol-heated floor of the next room. "You are a good man, Kyung Jae," she whispers close to his ear as she feels a deep, true sense of oneness with him.

---

6. *Ture/Doorae nongak.*

CHAPTER VIII

THE COMMUNITY HARVEST

K i Jun eagerly rises early after a good, deep sleep. He anticipates joining Young Kim and the village groups for the gathering of food from various locations in the Volunteer-labor village. All the food will be collected and taken to the house of one of the elder women members of the association. From there, most all the women villagers will work together at the festival site to prepare a common meal for the village. This is a time of co-operative-labor for the women.

The women love this time of co-operative labor for many reasons. Virtually all of them extremely enjoy singing together while they prepare the food. Each woman has her own personal reason why she likes this common-labor activity. Dan Bae likes to learn from stories about her son's generation and how they developed their respective talents and abilities. She also likes to listen to the women as they talk together. Even more, she likes to learn something new, how the women cook their own soup recipes for their families. She is widely respected for her own great skill in consistently serving delicious *soup/stew*[1]—the specific dish by which the Korean standard of culinary excellence is measured. She worked hard in her early years of marriage to learn from her mother-in-law how to expertly cook traditional, Korean soup/stew. So, she appreciates the opportunity to continue to learn from others.

Today, Ki Jun will see the women but for a brief time, since he has determined in his mind to work with and to talk to his musician counterpart, Young Kim. He is focused on plans of his agenda for the day at his morning meal as he sits at the table. Then, he reflects on the previous day's activities. He does not feel fully satisfied with his conversation with Young Kim about the S*pecialized Farmers Music and Dance band*[2] that they have both seen. He wants to talk more about the possibilities that the life of Specialized Farmers Music may offer—perhaps to both of the band leaders.

---

1. *chigae*
2. N*amsadang p'ae*

Now, he turns his attention back to breakfast and he jumps up quickly to begin to make rice, and then removes the cover from the big earthenware jar of *kimchee* [3]. He likes these two food staples for any meal, as they are easy to prepare, are nutritious, they always satisfy him and keep him full of energy. Occasionally, he enjoys a Western-style breakfast for the novel taste, or for the ease and quickness of opening a box of corn-flakes, bran, or some other cereal. He sometimes smiles at the sight of the Western-design package of corn flakes on his kitchen shelf, which brings to his mind the convenience—borrowed from another culture.

Ki Jun knows that the team will soon be going in groups to two separate locations to collect two varieties of food. Thus, the Farmers music team plans to play and dance en route from farm to farm. While they pick the food from the trees, which should take but little time at each of the farms, they will do some traditional, responsive singing, with Young Kim as lead singer. The band will enthusiastically sing joyful songs of thanks for another harvest of good, nourishing food. Young Kim will lead them in songs of appreciation for their beautiful 'jutting-finger' peninsula, strewn with mountainous beauty; *Chosun*, the Land of Morning Calm is a great homeland and cause about which they can sing with unrestrained zeal.

Young Kim loves to sing those songs, often. He tells the others that the songs of appreciation help him to work better and faster. He tells them that they must

---

3. Popular & famous Korean staple of spicy, marinated cabbage and turnips; traditionally made in large quantities and stored in large clay vessels in the ground for the winter.

acknowledge the Great One [4] for this productive spot on earth which provides a rich and diverse diet for all. All the members of the band acknowledge the yearly, abundant harvest of food. Especially, in a personal way, for the skills and abilities in music and dance which have been given to make their work so enjoyable. Such joyful times make it seem as if their shared labor activities were not work, at all.

Also, to these people, Volunteer-labor Association Farmers Music is a rare gift, not seen as a common thing, or a common part of life. It is to be, and is, valued as a gift from the special Gift-Giver.

Even so, for Young Kim, there exists such a subtle ease of the Farmers music band life that he sometimes does not regard the rich value that his life holds. Still, he takes part, sincerely, in the singing and dancing that he learned from his parents. This is a highly valued part of his inheritance.

Yet, now, to Young Kim and Ki Jun, there seems to be much else to be sought after. Both young men are exhilarated with the richness of life and the broad variety of choices that life is now seems to offer them. Young Kim expectantly hopes to talk to Ki Jun about these things, but he knows he now must turn his attention to the Farmers Band. The band has assembled, and singing, Young Kim leads them along the road, down the slowly curving bank of the rice paddy. This bank goes directly from Ki Jun's house to the house of Sub Won, one of the players of the small gong [5].

---

4. *Hananim*

5. *kwaenggwari*

He has asked the band to follow his lead in singing along the short way. They are joyful and ready, so they begin to sing, dance, stomp, twirl and jump high as they move along the road! Young Kim's enthusiasm is infectious, and he is exhilarated about what this day may reveal.

As the team arrives at Sub Won's house, Ki Jun thinks about the fruit trees on the farm of Sub Won, and he relishes the thought of eating the sweet and tasty Asian pears. Ki Jun knows Sub Won's pears are 'personally groomed' with great knowledge and care, and thus are well known in the entire village to always be delicious. They are appreciated so much that they are sometimes used as prizes in competitions. Competition winners are content with their rewards, which they usually begin to eat very soon after they have received them as a prize.

Ki Jun appreciates the pears' availability, and makes an acrobatic leap, which displays both his agility and *enthusiasm* [6]. The type of leap Ki Jun makes fascinates both young and old. In the dance, its quickness is dramatized when the musician's feet leave the ground, and spin in a complete 360-degree circle—like the hands of a clock! The feet would thus pivot all around the dancer's head, allowing him to land on the ground almost at the spot where he had departed.

Whenever such a maneuver is performed, such as Ki Jun's leap, the eyes of the children are usually fixed on the dancer's almost-unmoving head while he is 'airborne'. They respond with shouts of glee and awe. The amazed children also wonder how the head can just 'float in the air', while the body, legs, and feet whirl

---

6. *meut,* pronounced like 'mutt'

around in a haze. They supportively watch with a wondering, hopeful sincerity that won't allow the head to receive any harm. Admiration comes in a context of gymnastic-wonder of body-agility and discipline. What really evokes these feelings? It is that these dancers are dazzling in their skillfulness, and quickly become role models, though somewhat impractical, for the children. For Ki Jun, the joy of his first successful, solo leap is refreshed with each subsequent leap. And now, just as in that leap, he feels the exhilaration of the adrenaline coursing through his body. With satisfaction and anticipation, Ki Jun now begins to accelerate the tempo of the rhythm-keeping, small-gong. As his feet hit the ground, he simultaneously sounds the gong with the first beat of the stick.

The pace is thus set. The band naturally and easily follows his lead, while the large gong [7] player anticipates and echoes Ki Jun's first beat. Every member of the band is enthusiastic; one standard of the Common-labor bands, which allows them to perform beyond their own expectations of themselves.

Ki Jun's hat, according to tradition, is adorned with a 15-foot long, swivel-borne, paper streamer which swirls atop the hat—a replica of an ancient military hat. The streamer trails, swimming and floating far behind—and from side-to-side—of the musician's rhythmically nodding head. Like the long, floating streamer, the band dances along in a single, snaking line, as they follow the leader in their joyful, energetic, and determined procession of celebration.

---

7. *ching*-larger Farmers band gong, about one foot or more in diameter.

The band has inherited a patriotic spirit and a dedicated enthusiasm of gratefulness, which catalyzes their daily work activities. The musicians who play the *hourglass-drum*[8] — the native Korean instrument—shout a loud, gleeful punctuation to their joyful, ecstatic feeling, as they beat the double-headed instrument with a stick in each hand. The entire band gives and receives a unified shout, as a stimulus. It will be another day of productive village life, to serve both the needs of the village, and of one another.

Next, the band stops to play a tribute of thanks for the fruit they are about to harvest. Ki Jun will then proceed directly to the orchard of Asian pears which are ready to be picked. He hopes to pick rapidly, as he anticipates the rich and delicious savor of the fruit. Half of the group continues to dance and march behind Sub Won's farm to the neighboring farm where other fruit is waiting to be picked for the fall harvest. Apples are a 'latter day' favorite in Korea, as they were only introduced in modern times by American Presbyterians and Methodists missionaries. Those missionaries, who brought the Bible, also served as the literacy tool for the *common masses* [9], which comprised the majority of Korea's population.

Before that literary event in the late 1880's, only a minority of the educated elite were fully literate. They, usually upper class-noblemen and women, were usually literate in the Chinese language as well as in the almost-four-centuries-old Korean written language—'Hangul'. That was before the missionaries from the West 'invaded' Korean soil!

---

8. *changgu*
9. *Minjung*

This 'non-Korean factor' contributed to a 'social separation', wherein the direction of music diverged from the origins of the Volunteer-labor Association lifestyle. How did that separation take place? It began in the early part of the development of the Volunteer-labor associations, whereas centuries ago it was established that all community members would volunteer for the workload within the community — for the good of the village.

Eventually however, selective allocations developed due to farm size, amount of wealth and need, as well as a new sense of social status. There then arose an uncharacteristic, social division in villages, for so-called 'practical reasons', whereas previously, there had not been any such distinctions.

Still, here on the orchard-farm site, nearly everyone loves the foreign contribution. It is an addition of delicious variety to compliment the abundant, native produce. The healthful apple also was introduced to Korea by the hands of ones from outside—who helped to open the pages of ancient history and bring a continuation in Korea of the eternal saga of *Hananim*, the Great One.

A piece of fruit—the pear—is but a small item in the large, diverse, Korean diet. Yet, a number of common-labor team members shared the thought to themselves of the abundance of the area of planted orchards, and of the delicious crispness of this 'Korean ancestor'.

As several workers stand and reach to pick sweet pieces of fruit, each individual wonders, 'What difference does one, small, thing like this make? Is one item of food, the Asian pear, unique in its species of fruit, even when added to the selection at a harvest time such as this?' The addition is a small one, but it adds a significant change to the course of the land. Small? Yes. But it is greater, when one considers that this land became recognized by Westerners—by its long-time, isolationist label as 'The Hermit Kingdom', emerging as a country open to ideas from throughout the world.

'The Common populace; the God of Heaven; apples and pears . . . Are these associated 'concepts'?' Thoughts about these things occur simultaneously to both Young Kim and Ki Jun as they work at adjacent farm-sites, as they pick pears and apples for the much anticipated festival-celebration. These words together seem incoherent and abstract—yet, they are each an integral part of the nation's history.

At that moment, neither man is conscious that his thoughts have become sorted and ordered for the next dialogue. They will soon have this talk together, at the entire village's *common meal* [10]. Both men remain eager for that soon-approaching time!

The picking of fruit proceeds rapidly, as all the workers are eager to carry their fruit rapidly to the festival cooking area, located next to the Ture/Doorae *farm office* [11]. The villagers all anticipate a great meal, and a great day, that comes with a celebration of the entire village.

Like the others, Young Kim and Ki Jun are quick—and eager to work hard and fast to pick their respective fruit. When picking is completed, the two work-groups meet along the road. Some are tired, and all are dusty. The first group remains by the apple orchard, and turns toward their destination, while the approaching group falls-in behind the first group as it moves along the road.

---

10. The '*wet chori*'.

11. *nong chong.*

The groups have synchronized their timing, so that the latter group does not even come to a complete stop to let the 'pear-picking group' march by before them. As they march and dance along the road, the two young men acknowledge one another with slight bows and large smiles. They do not hesitate or stop, however, for they know they will soon have an opportunity to talk at length. That will be as soon as the groups arrive to deposit their fruit at the preparation point for the big feast.

The group members are exhilarated, and they feel almost intoxicated! Included in that state are two young *Farmers music and dance* [12] leaders, who share a great joy. Now, the band, together with a small number of the Volunteer-labor team, sings and dances along the road as they return with the produce. Young Kim sings loudly, with enthusiasm, as the others accompany and follow his lead.

The 'A-frame' backpacks of the laborers are filled high with what each man has picked. These load-carriers with horizontal supports of branches seem not to hinder the bearers as they skip, leap and even twirl along the road.

The villagers are mostly all well-aware of the great value of mutual labor. And, they know of the valuable potential of the co-operative effort, and the subsequent, correspondent co-operative gain.

This village labor group is being knit together in harmony, not only by the music, but also by the shared labor, and the processionally dancing farmers. The group is nearing the end of the present phase of the task. With

12. *Nongak.*

great anticipation of the upcoming event, each heart is pumping with a 'co-operative and joyful anticipation'.

Those men who are ready to carry the produce for the cook crew meet at the office building, and lift the 'A-frame' backpacks from the backs of the workers. They empty those packs into large, wooden vats which have been placed outside the Volunteer-labor office. The women then gather the food for preparation.

Two to three hundred gallons of fresh apples and pears are ready to be prepared. The women at the Volunteer-labor office are enthused, especially because they have planned their work well. They continue to sing as they are about to prepare the remaining half of the fruit for salads and compotes.

Young Kim and Ki Jun are very familiar with the routine of this special day; the Special Common-Meal day. They know that after the entire village has enjoyed the big meal, that they will have a time of Farmers band service, with music and dancing. The whole village will be involved. Then, everybody will have a good rest.

Both men know that this is not a regularly scheduled work day, so there will be more time for them to make plans. And, they know that the specialized farmers music experience that they've had has affected them, and perhaps others, as well.

Two young brothers empty their A-frame backpacks of their loads of fruit and go over by a large tree and sit in its shade. They are members of the Volunteer-labor team who have been picking fruit. Both are about the same age as Young Kim and Ki Jun. Like the other two, they have watched the *Specialized Farmers Music Band* [13] perfor-

---

13. *Namsadang p'ae*

mance. They also enjoyed the performance, and they are now engaged in serious thought and talk about that topic.

"If you were in a Farmers music band, do you think you would ever consider joining one of those troupes of strolling actors like the one that we saw?" asks the first brother, the older of the two.

"How can I answer that question?" answers the second brother. "You know that according to the tradition of our Volunteer-labor village, and even almost the whole nation, we do not make a decision separate from the group. I would have to have the agreement of our family, at least. And you know that would include your consent, too. Or, after the family's decision, I would be accountable to the Volunteer-labor Association representatives, or the elders."

"I agree," the older brother says, confirming his younger sibling.

"We still make our decisions like our ancestors have been doing for such a long time. Some Koreans now have adapted to modern, Western ways. They make their own decisions, without regard to the well being of the whole group. I cannot imagine living in that manner.

"I would feel so isolated and so alone making decisions without seeking others' advice or agreement," the second brother again agrees with the first.

"Yes, it would not be easy to decide 'the modern way', so independently." Clearly, the two brothers are in agreement. "I am happy that I am not a Farmers Music Band member. I would not want to be tempted to join a group like the Specialized Farmers Music group that we saw, yesterday.

"Neither would I want to have to ask my family let me go away with a group of strangers. They would not allow, so easily, a family member to just leave! How could we leave our family—or village, behind?

"And, my thoughts and feelings on this subject are not determined merely by our culture. Rather, they are deeply rooted in our faith. For, in the family of our ancestors' God, we are united as members of His family. Like our national tradition, although we might not always see the results of our actions, our actions as the children of God always affect the entire family. Rarely are there individual choices that do not affect everyone else in some way—great or small. It might be easier for a Farmer Music Band member to adopt the modern, individualistic way, but . . ."

"This common meal will be delicious," declares the elder, first brother. "The food tastes better to me when I know that I have helped to pick it from the field." The younger brother agrees with that, with a broad smile.

"Yes, and it tastes better, too, when I know that those who eat with me also have worked to help provide the meal. The food should be ready soon. Let us go to see if they need more charcoal for the barbeques, or wood for the rice pot. We'll help to be sure everybody will get enough *barbequed beef* and the delicious *ribs*."[14]

The brothers rise and go to offer aid to the cooperative-labor cooking team. Their help is needed for just a small amount of work, but their contribution helps things run more efficiently, as they bring more firewood for the giant cauldron. The women continue to sing in unison as they begin to serve the food to everyone waiting in line,

---

14. (a) *pulgogi*, beef.

(b) *kalbi,* pork ribs. This and 14a are two of the most popular meat staples in the Korean diet.

from the big, boiling cauldrons. The people are standing in a line, happily talking as they wait in their place and move forward to where the food is served.

Each person is served as they pass the serving tables, and take their large bowls from a young man, the server, who must work rapidly to keep up. From there, they go to the big cauldrons, where rice is scooped into their bowls with a large ladle, and so on with the rest of the food in the service line.

The action of 'eating rice from the same cauldron', as the farmers always say, brings a sense of unity and bonding to everyone eating from the large, black, steaming, iron cauldrons. To appear at the cauldron is almost monumental, and also serves much like a giant magnet to draw people together in a moment of unified stillness. After getting their large bowls of rice, meat, and *kim chee*, the people walk and find places on nearby benches, among surrounding clusters of trees, or on large, bench-like rocks. The atmosphere is happy and warm, as the village of Suwon-san once again resembles a large family, reunited for a joyous celebration.

CHAPTER IX

FARMER MUSIC, REST, FUTURE PLANS

"This *kim chee* [1] is delicious, Young Kim," Ki Jun says. "With the rice, and barbequed beef, it should make me *very* energetic for our music and dance session, after we eat. This good food will be great fuel for the unquenchable joy needed to dance the best that I can.

---

1. A Korean staple of spiced, marinated turnips, turnip greens and/ or cabbage.

135

"It will be the fuel needed for the *enthusiasm* [2] and *style* [3] that we all need to dance the Farmers dance correctly." All that Young Kim could say was to answer, "Yes." His concise answer proved his love for the hot barbeque, rice, and kim chee. He smiles his agreement to Ki Jun as he vigorously chews his food. "Yes," he repeats. Ki Jun returns a knowing smile.

The minds of the two young men again are in accord. As they scan the crowded area with their eyes, they see small clustered groups of families and friends, busily enjoying the delicious meal together. The people are clustered in small and larger groups, here and there. They are mostly situated under the scattering of tall trees, which provides a refreshing blend of cool shade, and warm sunlight.

The two men look across the grounds at the many clusters of people eating. They know that soon, here on this ground, they will get the opportunity to serve the whole village, while exceptionally enjoying the time. Young Kim and Ki Jun continue to look at the landscape with an evaluation of the surface of the land as being relatively hard and level. Each man silently reflects on the surface as very good for dancing and jumping. They see that there is much open space to run, jump and freely turn, without concern for the hindrance of rocks, trees, or embankments. The band members are preparing themselves emotionally, even as they eat together. Now, they are prepared to actively celebrate!

---

2. *meut.*

3. *heung-* To have that 'something extra', a motivating force that helps them to happily dance and sing, and play their instruments better than ever before.

Young Kim finishes his meal while Ki Jun continues to eat, very energetically! Young Kim practices two songs by humming them silently, which in a short time he will sing as the band plays and dances. Young Kim also considers the length of time necessary for the band to prepare and change into their band regalia.

For himself, Young Kim is already wearing his white shirt and pants, and his colored sash. He only needs to get his hat and colored shoulder sash. His energy and emotions have now reached the highest level. He sees himself as a cooking container; ready to boil liquids, and then 'to whistle itself into relation with the container's user'! He knows that Ki Jun only needs to get his swivel-streamer hat and his *small gong,* [4] to be completely ready. Ki Jun finishes eating, in what seemed like so much time to Young Kim. Ki Jun is absorbed in the meal and thoroughly enjoying the time, as well as the selected and delicious, traditional food. He reflects to himself for a short moment of his appreciation of the women's Ture Festival Team. If only by the force of habit, he is still very thankful for them.

As the two *Nongak* band members return their dishes by the *Ture* building, some of the people move in the direction of a clearing, a treeless area, to get a good place to view the *Farmers Band Music and Dance* [5] performance. Everyone anticipates this event as a special after-eating reward. An almost universal principle, to eat a meal together causes the people to feel more closely akin to one another. The ties of family in farm labor music are traditional and consistently observed by poorer farmers.

---

4. *kwaenggwari*

5. *Nongak*

Many of those who know this fact are happy to be identified with those ancestors who endured impossible circumstances. Yet, on this occasion, Young Kim and Ki Jun are not among that group, for their hearts now yearn to experience new adventure and glory. Their thoughts turn away from all they have. Their focus is on what they do not have, and what they want. Still, their own consciences whisper of correct methods and procedures of the Volunteer-labor association community. The two men have intoxicated themselves with the Specialized Farmers Music experience. They have not even considered the mandatory requirement that their request to leave the Common-labor Association Community be reviewed by the community.

One by one, the band members happily and contentedly pass into the room at the back of the community office. This is a special room where the hoes are kept, according to tradition. On the first day of work, the tools are brought to that room. Just as each following day, they are stored there for the night. There is private ownership of these relatively inexpensive items, yet they are stored and kept as a community resource.

Likewise, on the last day of the work season, the whole team will wash their hoes and then take them home until the beginning of the next season of work. Then, they will again begin the dedication and storage process.

Both the first and the last days of the work season involve a celebration where the people come together in thanksgiving and enjoy a festive meal together. Those days are eagerly anticipated for the celebration, as well as for a number of other reasons. A festive spirit now fills the room as the band eagerly prepares for the performance.

The band members prepare quickly, excitedly, and file out the door with a rush of wind. The association's officers who are not part of the Farmers band, nevertheless, lead the band out into the bright sunlight. They bear the standards, which display the unique identity of this Volunteer-labor group which desires to achieve an identity of social and economic accountability.

The large banner [6] is placed at the front of the line, at the head of the dance area. The first officer plants its poles firmly in the dense soil, and then turns to stand and give an admiring salute-like glance. He cries out with a joyful shout when he realizes within himself the rare beauty of this identifying banner.

It reads; FARMING—ORDAINED BY THE GREAT ONE—IS THE WORK-GIFT TO THE WORLD.

He is familiar with the creation story, so he reflects that farming was the original task of humanity. Still, he knows that in the very beginning work was not the same toil of sweat, tears and pain that it has become since 'the fall' of Original Sin.

The large banner floats and announces an acceptable extension of the ancient, traditional-historic Farmers music band signature. The smaller, colorful pennant follows close behind the large banner, as the band starts the procession. The small banner identifies this village's Volunteer-labor Farmers band, as unique from any other. The pennant is carried by the second officer, who plants its ploes in the ground near the larger banner.

---

6. *yonggi*

The festival of *Volunteer-labor Play* [7] proceeds, led by Ki Jun, who plays the small gong loudly, with good rhythm—and it is quite strong— enough to keep the whole band in unison. Young Kim follows. He leads the responsive singing and dancing. He jumps and twirls, pivoting his body through the air as he leans side-to-side. Then, he steps high with alternating legs. He is filled with uncontainable enthusiasm, which he expresses as best he can.

Young Kim begins to sing the popular favorite, "Working With Singing," accompanied by Ki Jun, who sets the rhythm with his gong. This song typifies the persistent, enduring character of Volunteer-labor association Farmers music and dance band working members. Those who dance behind came in a file simulating a military march. Then, spontaneously and fluidly, the band breaks into an acrobatic marching-dance, with individuals swirling about in 360 degree spins, which reflect the leader's enthusiasm. The band members jump with their colorful sashes and belts flying loose and free around them, singing their responses, in unison, to the leader's call.

The group's enthusiasm is stimulated even more by the beating of the larger gong that is sounded by band members who weave themselves in and out among the other members. The large gong players strike the gongs.

The *large gong's* [8] penetrating ring and resounding sound stimulates the worker's collective excitement here at the festival, just as it does in day-to-day fieldwork.

---

7. *Ture/Doorae nori*
8. *ching*

The Farmers music band plays and dances for an extended period of time, just as they do at every Volunteer-labor Farmers Play and Feast day. They play through the rest-for-all time, since such rest-fellowship harmonizes well with the relaxing pleasure of eating together. While others rest, the band does not lose their enthusiasm. They exert their energy with jumping and making rhythmic percussive melodies to echo their joyful singing.

The music of encouragement causes the festival-goers to rest with contentment and be happy to celebrate this day as a village unit. The celebration of their successful collective farm and market system is rooted in the beliefs and traditions of their pioneer ancestors. It was a heritage of priceless value, considered a privilege and opportunity to celebrate this day.

As the band plays light rhythms, Young Kim steps aside to rest and to allow his traditional replacement to take his place and lead the responsive singing. While he also enjoys his hard-earned rest, he enjoys that he can hear, from a distance, the quality sound of his band's music. Young Kim gives particular notice to his band as a symbol of the social cohesiveness of the village's government. This value is all too often sought after and not attained among the multitudes of the people. Those multitudes, *the commoners* [9], are so called throughout Korean history.

An emotional bond is being made in the hearts of the people, and through the spiritual bond, it is made deeper, still. The band now splits into two groups after the exchange of lead singers has taken place. The two bands face one another and begin to sing in alternating rounds.

---

9. *Minjung*

The music produced is especially resonant because the distance between the bands creates an ideal mingling of sound. At the same time, drama players begin to review the drama they are about to perform for the village. They sing joyful songs and thanksgiving songs. The songs they sing are all carefully chosen for this day. There are songs to the God of their ancestors—who is *the Great One* [10]. They sing to their God who made and provides all things.

The band also sings the classic 'Good Harvest Song' with great enthusiasm. Following that song is 'Peace of the World', another classic, Common-labor, Farmers Band song. The third and last song to be performed by the two groups is sung responsively and in rounds. The last song is the much loved song, 'The Song of the Farmers', which has been sung on the farms since before precise memory.

Rest time is almost complete when Young Kim notices the movement of his father. Young Kim has arisen just as Kyung Jae rose up from a place on the large bench made from a split pine log. Young Kim's eyes are fixed upon his father as he walks to near the front of the line of band members. His father has just arisen from the same place where he, Young Kim, had rested, only a few minutes earlier.

So, Young Kim watches his father walk, and he walks from where his mother is sitting. Then, he proceeds a short distance from that clearing of trees. Something unknown causes Young Kim to look intently at his father. Unexpectedly then, Young Kim notices a very sad look

10. *Hananim*

on his father's face. After having relaxed to the heart-and soul-warming melodies he just heard-and played, Young Kim's body now becomes tense. The extreme change in circumstances is a sudden and shocking surprise.

The image of his father's face burns into Young Kim's mind and heart. Instantly, he knows that he must act quickly to remedy the situation.

With his heart screaming, Young Kim first has to learn the cause of this horror, and then find a way to bring quick comfort!

"This sadness seems to penetrate my father's whole being," Young Kim thinks. "I will go without delay and give my father some comfort." In his haste, he does not realize the naiveté of his situation.

Still, he realizes what the time is and the place is, and he withholds himself from rushing forward, unrestrained. Instead, he thinks to himself that he will create a new song in his heart, spontaneously, to calm and soothe his own mind.

"Then," he thinks, "that gross image on my father's face will disappear, and from my mind, as well." With that relief, he continues to reason to himself, 'I will be better able to understand the problem which has so fiercely attacked my father, and what I might do to bring him some relief.'

Young Kim begins to do, by habit, what has helped him gain the coveted position of lead singer in the band. That is, he seeks for inspiration to create. And then he will sing what he has so quickly created, by opening his heart to The One who has inspired great music from the beginning. The song is on the tip of his tongue, so Young Kim assumes an attitude of celebration and begins to sing with enjoyment of this, the collective Farming and music lifestyle.

He sings;

We work together,
And the produce is efficient. Yea! It is so-o-o-o good. Yea! It is great. And greater than—
When a farmer works alone.
We work together. With our music, we have pleasant exercise.

We work together, and the outcome
Belongs to Him who provides it.
So we use the gift of agriculture—
And we thank and honor the Bestower.

Yea! We thank and honor the Great One.

Smiles appear on the faces of any of those who are close enough to hear Young Kim's song, including the band members. And, joy appears on his face, too. During his rest time Young reflects. 'How good,' he thinks—that nobody has actually laid back to rest before everybody has finished eating his or her own meal. Each person has waited for all to finish before proceeding to 'the next phase'. All the people appreciate the order as an intrinsic part of the Volunteer-labor farm-life. In that, Young Kim deeply appreciates another function of his life inheritance.

Young Kim has not made the connection of this appreciation with his earlier thoughts of the imagined glory of leaving his home village with Ki Jun to travel with a small group of strolling actors.[11] He feels confident, and in his mind there is, therefore, no conflict. It was a dream, nevertheless.

The drama players begin to assemble as they walk to the clearing where the band has previously danced and played. Then, they quickly organize themselves and begin the drama.

As they begin, Young Kim's attention instinctively shifts to his father once again, to the place where he had seen him with a forlorn look, so removed from his usual character of liveliness. With that, the image of his father's pained face reappears in his mind's eye.

So, he walks warily toward his father, with each step considering what could be the cause of such pain. And why? Then suddenly, without understanding why, the vitalized refreshing he had from the drama performance begins to slip away.

"Father, hello!" says Young Kim, gently. He tries to conceal anything other than the joy that he thinks his father might expect at any moment. "Yes," he responds, "your performance was very good." Kyung Jae tries to cover the deep, previously felt sadness.

His attempt to cover-up is very unsuccessful, much like his own son's attempt to conceal his true feelings, so as to not add to his father's apparent pain. The two quickly lock glances upon one another's eyes. Then, they share an instantaneous acknowledgement of discomfort, mutually seen by each man.

"May I speak very directly to you, father?" Young Kim asks. His father nods his consent with his head tilted

---

11. *Namsadang p'ae*

low. "What is it that has upset you? Is it me, or us, that is the cause of this problem?

"Have we not performed in a manner that can bring respect and honor to our Farmer band, to this collective-labor community, to our family and to the God of Heaven? Is it not to Him that we must give honor, before all else? Honor to Him who has given us all that we have harvested and will also enjoy, so much?"

Kyung Jae feels so deeply touched with an inner sorrow, that he is not easily able to communicate to his son, Young.

Young Kim's mind, likewise, is burdened with varied emotionally impacting events of the exciting, previous twenty- four hours.

Kyung Jae's desire is to protect his son from the shock of a communication, which he, himself, has just received from a passerby, a communication which shot a stunning numbness into him. Only an hour before, a neighbor wandered by where Kyung Jae sat and told him of the report from the hospital. A critical injury was the tragic result of the accident that occurred earlier—of which many in two villages knew all about.

The gentleness in which Kyung Jae had wanted to wrap this article of news was hidden by the pain of the burden of having to repeat and spread the sorrowful news. Kyung Jae's eyes are becoming slightly moist, and at that moment he cannot lift his eyes to look his son in the face.

"There is double the bad news in one report, Young Kim," his father adds, his voice trembling. "The two men from the next village, who wanted to initiate a two-village, Volunteer-labor Farmers association and band, were the two who were put in critical condition, Young Kim . . ." He stops speaking, for he cannot continue.

"No!" cries Young Kim. He blindly grasps at his father's sleeves for balance. "Then, Chong Won and Hong Won . . ." Young Kim questions, "are they also like being without fathers?" Young Kim feels dizzy. He steadies himself, clutching more tightly to his father's upper arms. The two men stand together, silently. Neither is able to speak, nor was there any place for thoughts. The state of shock is all they are able to share.

Young Kim instantly realizes that the village, which is already in need of much help, has now tragically added two boys and a little sister to the already excessive list of unprotected or orphaned children.

The two boys loved the men who had been seriously injured. They share the understanding that real love simply wants the best for the recipient of that love. They love these men about as much as they did the co-laborers from their own village, just as they also love the children of the injured pair.

Kyung Jae leans momentarily against his son for stability. Then he instinctively leans back against the tree that is close behind him and pulls his son close to himself. He does this to prevent his faltering body from falling. Both men have a special affection and a special hope for the stricken men and their boys—and the little girl.

Young Kim releases his father's arm. Then his gaze turns out to the distance. The path of his eyes crosses the lonely figure of his mother, who sits not far from the two most important men in her life.

Now, neither man moves nor speaks, as the significance of the loss and the pain related to the relationships involved reach their hearts. Both father and son are literally staggered and overwhelmed. They can do nothing but stand captive—each man being bewildered and stunned like animals suddenly thrust into a confining cage.

Thoughts of shattered lives and broken plans, and the thought of the three small children demand an active place in the minds of both men, simultaneously. The children, who lost a parent at least temporarily, are already children of fathers whose own wives they had previously lost.

The two seriously injured single fathers had joined in partnership with Kyung Jae and the village to organize a new Volunteer-labor Farmers work force as an inter-village group.

The Farmers music and dance band was a required part of the active group to be established in the village adjacent to Suwon-san. The new group was meant to be joined by Kyung Jae's Volunteer-labor work force on a limited, but totally committed, basis.

But, two critical and necessary human elements had now been all but removed, which were two of the best workers of Suwon-san's neighbor village. These thoughts now activated deep sorrow—that of damaged love and unrealized potential. This now floods the emotions of both the father and the son. The two still do not speak, as they stand motionless in their sorrowful shock.

Kyung Jae and Young Kim stand as if under a personal and deliberate attack. Near them sits Dan Bae, also nearly transfixed by sadness. The feeling of loss is the unfortunate connection of the family members.

Many lives have been changed. Both villages are changed significantly—at least for an indefinite time, and with all untimeliness.

What *had* seemed to be like the sprouting of the blossom of new hope for a suffering village has *now* changed to an unexpected uprooting of that fresh, fragile blossom. The blossom is now uprooted and crushed. So seemed the circumstances to many interested ones to whom the sad report was made.

The loss—at least temporarily—of the fathers, workers and liaison people from the village would demand sacrifices from any self-centered desires, and perhaps a significant, compensatory re-ordering of life patterns. These individuals are almost fully aware of the reality, but it will soon become much clearer to them.

The two injured men were 'critical links' between the villages, which now are broken. The uprooted and crushed blossoms are now becoming a symbol of broken lives and hopes. Many in each of the two villages are keen to do something extreme—even revolutionary. The plan encompasses them finding a social and economic, even a spiritual breakthrough, in conciliation.

The untimeliness of this tragedy is dramatic for those whose vision is of social and spiritual growth for the two villages, and for the families directly affected by the accident.

As Kyung Jae and his son stand amidst the festivities, within themselves, they are still isolated and emotionally far from the environment around them. It is as if they are alone in a partially secluded wooded area. And, their beings remain numbed to the external environment.

They become detached from those surrounding them by virtue of their preoccupation with this issue of the heart. Standing motionless after all this time, the men seem almost as if dead and deaf to all the sounds around them. Their afflicted ears hear only muted sounds, and there is no contact with reason—for a time, as sorrow casts its looming shadow.

The men cannot even question within themselves if there is anything to be done to alleviate the pain-of-loss that must be shared by both villages. To an observer, the two men seemed to be taking it hard. Nevertheless, they do not put their hopes in circumstances, but in greater things.

Neither Kyung Jae nor Young Kim really knows how long ago the play-day drama by the Volunteer-labor group was completed. But, they both then realize that the drama team had left without notifying them of their departure. The two men now find themselves together— as if being awakened from a dream. Again, they become aware that they are isolated much like they had been when the tragic news of the serious injuries was reported.

The Farmers music band is no longer playing, and they begin to disperse among the thinning mass of village participants.

Much time passed before Kyung Jae 'came to his senses'. He is now able to re-assume his natural character trait of spontaneous action. Still, he is just able to begin to communicate his real thoughts and feelings to Young Kim. Kyung Jae and Young Kim face options, realized by the functional loss of the sole living parents of the three small children. The children have lost their natural, parental protection and are left vulnerable for the immediate future.

Kyung Jae thought it more than coincidence that some elders of the village next to Suwon-san had made tentative plans to organize a more substantial collective-labor group to support the large number-by-ratio, of orphaned children. That village had a high number of orphaned children compared to its total population.

The elder community members and some others want to work in the collective-labor association, to help bear the load. Their intention is especially so that they might help stimulate needed agricultural productivity in the community. They will also be enabled to better support themselves and the orphans without a decrease in total productivity.

Finally, Kyung Jae speaks to his son. "Young Kim, the life we live here is good. You know that I have always been thankful for that. It is not an accident, nor a coincidence. We are inheritors of many valuable gifts from heaven, especially one immeasurably great gift.

"The origin of that gift is love. It is like the root. The tree's root is a source of life of a tree full of ripe fruit. There were ancient farmers who were forced to turn their backs on faith in the Divine One, the God of even *their* ancestors. They believed that farming was the gift ordained from heaven, so long ago.

That is the inspiration for the ancient practice of proclaiming our divine inheritance of farming. The tradition of our large banner, our '*yonggi*', which tells of our earthly occupation, has come from the same, ancient source. Because of the ancient, imperial sanction from China, they were prevented from documenting in writing that farming came from *Hananim*, or God, but only that it came from a divine source!"

"That idea does not make logical sense to me, father," Young Kim answers.

"I cannot see the sense in it either, Young," his father agrees. "What I believe is that farming is not the complete gift that was given. Still, farming is not a thing to be taken for granted. To do farm work with a heart for the people and for the land is a very important part of correctly receiving the gift."

CHAPTER X

A GIFT TO BE RECEIVED

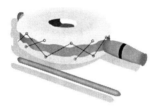

K yung Jae is amazed that his words seem to leap from his lips as he continues to talk with his son. "The responsibility of not taking the divine gift for granted is something that has been lost in many places throughout the world, as well as in many village locations in this country. That gift was given to us partly for an example. When our ancestors and all the people of China were forbidden to pray to the God of Heaven/ *Hananim*, both they, *and we*, became as lost from Him, just like we were absolutely separated. That is the best evaluation I can make.

"Young Kim, it is as if all of us have lost all of our own fathers," Kyung Jae laments to his son. "It would be impossible for that to happen, as no man would exist, in that case. The Great One was grieved to have lost the love and companionship that He once had with these, his people, whom we call our ancestors. He then saw us as his orphans, just as we see the little ones in the next village.

"Of course, orphans need protection and love, so He sent his Son, the Godman, to earth. We know that the legendary founder of this nation, *Tangun*, is a type of the Godman. The true Godman came down here to earth to show every one of us the love of his Father. In the Son, we see the love for ones who have become orphans.

"Again, the Father is the Great One, whom we call "*Hananim*"!

"We have learned how to employ the gift, for now, as we favor widows, orphans, the weak, and the infirm, here in our village.

"Of the many good practices that they have done, *that* was one good thing practiced by the common-labor villages of generations long ago. Not all gifts that were given were received for good use," Kyung Jae says. "Just as the God of Heaven adopted us as orphans, so now, we too are able to be representatives of the parents lost by the orphans of the next village. We are now *'adoptive, Collective-labor Association parents'*."

Amazed, Kyung Jae is now surprised at the depth of his words, and he continues, "Before the accident, we discussed an option with Hong Won and Chong Won's father. If the village was not in favor of the mutual-labor group, then we were given an option."

As Young Kim simply studies his father's face, he's not sure he has fully handled the deep sorrow of the tragic news of the injuries. So, he waits for his father to continue to speak.

Kyung Jae does speak, "You know, Young Kim, in our culture, there is an inheritance of values and traditions that are very, very old. We have chosen many important values of our forefathers because the other choice is to reject values altogether—which ends in chaos and confusion—or to choose not to believe in the Great One, as some of the ancient ones of this land have done. The latter choice leads to exalting humanism or naturalism, both of which lead to making gods of man, materials or the state."

"Yes father, the war that divided our land was incited and fought by ones who call man a god. Then, they caused so many of the people to die who are little different than the very ones they idolize.

"Father, they were able to kill and oppress the ones who did not agree with the value that the material world is god," Young Kim suggests. His father agrees. "That is the sake for which much genocide across the world has been perpetrated by the 'man/state-is-god, the ideal being Utopian Socialism." So, the father clarifies his son's point.

"That system has always failed and never succeeded," Young Kim agrees with his father. "Why did they choose killing their own, rather than negotiating peace with them? We will have true national re-unification when they will do that."

"I agree, Young Kim," Kyung Jae answers. "You are right about our values and traditions. Just as here in our village, so throughout the nation, the 'koinonia' village system, or group-based decision system is designed to operate for people who follow the plan of *Hananim*, our

God. I am sorry to say that the Western influence has had some corrupting effects on the group-centered community," he continues. "In the West, people are more individualistic, and independent of one another.

"Now, more than ever, our youth and some older ones are taking the liberty of making independent decisions which reduces the fabric of our society, like it has never been done before," the father instructs. "They will not consult with the elders, or with others," Kyung Jae says, a little indignant. He now begins to show a fresh sign of revitalization of his emotions.

"Young Kim, I hope you can understand this. Recently, Korea, and the world have been experiencing new ways whose origins are influences of the Western culture. That culture also includes what is called 'modernism'. In the Western culture, people, are seeking their fortunes, more and more, by their individual minds and strength. It was not always that way. I understand that even in Western culture, in the past, people would seek the counsel of others. The movement of society shows that they are turning from that, and even some from the wise counsel of *Hananim*! Through the writing of God's most wise man, Solomon, He directs everybody to seek the counsel of many godly ones, before making important decisions. That is the safe way, Young Kim.

"Independence like that has never been the rule in Korea, but always the exception." Kyung Jae hesitates briefly to collect his thoughts and to listen to what is being spoken within. "In this land, we have overcome great problems by making decisions regarding our Common-labor village relationship with the next village. They now have several orphans, and a new, deeper and more urgent need for care, from us.

"As a leader in a Common-labor community, and as your father, I would like to ask you something that is important to me and important to you also, as you will see" his father says directly to his son. "First, do you think you would be willing and favor the option of our own collective Farmers music and dance team to begin to donate a limited amount of time to help the next village care for the orphans of their village? Our responsibility would be to do a certain amount of work in the fields to help them lighten the overload on those who have adopted children, as well as those who may adopt. Everybody knows the need for the second group now arises.

"It is important to us that you would be willing to help; and important to Suwon-san." He speaks to his son gently and without forbearance in his voice. Kyung Jae speaks from a point of shared responsibility with his son—not exclusive authority over his son. "Your talent and abilities will be used not only to bring encouragement and *enthusiasm* [1] to our labor teams, but to both of the villages whose relationship develops in a surprising way.

"More importantly, Young Kim, you will be a key member of the team, which can demonstrate many good things to the elders and the rest of the next village. We both know that our neighbors know something of our lifestyle, being the closest village to ours. And, to face the responsibility to have to re-order the living habits of an entire village, demands more than knowledge from an external location. Young Kim, it must be a natural part of their lives for them to understand well enough to make

---

1. *Meut.*

right decisions. Then, our commitment will be to the orphans, to their new parents, and to the entire village."

"Father, I'm sorry, but I think this is something to which I cannot give an immediate response," Young Kim says. "New ideas, experiences, and challenges seem to come in groups. I am considering some new things, which is something different from working on a volunteer-labor team, and with a Common-labor Music and Dance Band, in Suwon-san. But, I will say now that both of the questions that you propose are good—they seem like the right thing to do, and I cannot think of anything better that can be done."

Kyung Jae ponders his son's words. Then, he looks far away and waits for his son to stand, and to let his sorrowful emotions run their deep course. He takes a deep breath of the fresh, pine-scented air outside the Common-labor office. He simply grieves for the village next to Suwon-san, and he grieves for the extended families, as well as the children and the victims themselves. He offers thanks in his heart to heaven for the good number of years he has lived, and that he, himself, had never lost a close loved one in any tragic way.

Now, Young Kim is deeply moved. He slowly enters the office and in numbness leaves his hat, belt, and sashes in their respective places. Now unburdened, he begins to reflect on the events of the day. During the short while since his father's music and dance analogy, he has taken the opportunity to reconsider the influences of the previous day.

Then, he hears the band; a news-like report of Suwon-san, and musical comfort for the questions that challenge his preconceived ideas. The sound of the band stimulates Young Kim's thought. Young Kim and

Ki Jun are truly being diverted by the excitement of the new musical lifestyle they have seen together. But now, despite a great infatuating temptation, they cannot so easily decide to make a simple decision to join a troupe of strolling minstrels and actors—a 'specialized farmers music and dance band'!

Young Kim continues to reflect, and vividly remembers the true and good social values they have learned. He knows that he—no; both he *and* Ki Jun—cannot break tradition and their code of respect, without a prick of the conscience. He knows as well that to do so would abort social custom.

No, he realizes, it will not be that easy for them. He feels in his heart that if he does not seek the counsel of his family and the many villagers with whom he shared life and work, it will be a truly shameful thing. He and they actually work *for* one another! No, others could integrate Western values of individualism without accountability for the purpose of escaping the familiar, but he is now convinced that Ki Jun would agree with him that they could not.

Young Kim just processes these thoughts, but he isn't actively acknowledging, nor internalizing, their importance. He knows that who he is as a member of this subculture that lives for the good of the whole community first, then the individual—*that* is the identity that he can, and must claim! He reasons that group values and individual values are not mutually exclusive. He realizes that for him, it is a question of 'both-and'—not 'either-or'.

A word occurs to Young Kim as if from the sky. 'Voluntary'—that is the essence-word of a free society,' he thinks. Every member of such a society must give up the right to act independently of and non-accountable to the group. 'There are few exceptions,' he thinks. Young Kim remembers this as he watches people move about in the distance, talking joyfully and moving to the rhythmic sound of the band's music. The essence of Volunteer/ Common-labor is now what his mind focuses upon.

'The word 'common' is a difficult one for those with 'non-commoner heritage' is the thought that plays and replays in his mind. Yet, in this context, the word does not imply *mean* or *typical*. Contrarily, it refers to the non-distinction of rank which would (otherwise) bring social divisions. Generally, the non-distinction is necessary to clarify *relationship*, in and of the work produced *for* each member, since there must be some organizational rank to effectively administer labor, etc. Automatically and instantly, he is careful to block any idea of 'absolute' non-class distinction as an ideal — a foundational value the government of the North holds.

So, Young Kim thinks that a voluntary effort to serve, without thinking and acting for the good of the whole community, i.e. *Collective-labor* would not truly be Collective-labor. Again, he realizes that by natural, human, values, collective-labor cannot be more than simply human. 'This is simple thinking!' he realizes. 'But, *only* when applied in Kingdom terms — in heavenly language and with *kingdom* thinking, can this lifestyle effectively work! Otherwise, it is little different than communism!'

With these thoughts, Young Kim laughs at himself — in amazement, not in a self-demeaning way — that unexpected, self-imposed limits *are* possible. This timely laughter helps him to overcome, at least for the time, the heaviness and grief he experienced not too long ago. Young Kim walks only a few steps in the fresh, pine-scented air, and then he stops where his father stands alone. Abruptly, a wave of humility washes over him and he speaks to his father with spontaneous gentleness. "Father, I have found answers to my own problems in the midst of the other people's problems.

"I would like you to know how much I appreciate you, father," he says, as he measures out each word.

"Your experience and example of right character have helped me to see that I began to walk along another path. It is the path that leads to self-satisfaction, rather than trying hard to live a fulfilled life. There is a great, but subtle difference, I now realize! Fulfillment is the effect—the result—of our Volunteer-association lifestyle.

"Most of all, I would like to say, "Thank you, father."

Kyung Jae's heart opens through his son's words, and he begins to be filled with joy and appreciation. He is only a little uneasy at his son's directness. He has experienced such awkward directness from time to time, therefore, he is not too uncomfortable.

"Young Kim," his father answers, "your words are a great contribution to me, now. Especially, since I am increasing in years, as I am. I will say that as your father, at this time in my life, I appreciate your words more than ever. Many rewards of being your father have been realized since you have become more responsible for yourself and your own life. Because you said this to me, it is as a sweet, cool drink in a desperate and lonely time; just as it would be for a man lost at sea and alone.

"Now, especially, Young Kim, your words are so comforting. Now—when there is a new challenge for us in these two villages. It is so good to hear your appreciation of me, your father," Kyung Jae says, still a little affected by the burden of the disaster.

"You are welcome, father," Young Kim says, now smiling. "Will you call the Common-labor association meeting, soon, father?" Young Kim asks.

"Further consideration causes me to decide that today is not a good day to call an unexpected meeting without the elders' agreement, Young Kim," his father answers. "Tomorrow will also be a difficult time for many, due to the work schedule.

"I will call for a short, emergency meeting, tonight only, for representatives of each family of the village. After the meeting, they will report to their families, so that all may be told of the news and decisions made in the meeting about Suwon-san and the next village."

"This could be difficult for you, father. But, just as our ancestors did in millennia past, before the Imperial ban on prayer, I will pray to the God of Heaven, *Hananim*. I will pray that you have peace in your heart. And, I will pray for courage for you to successfully lead our collective-labor association representatives with much wisdom."

Young Kim hopes to see Ki Jun, despite the strong emotions with which he has wrestled. Expectantly, he says, "I can go to see Ki Jun. I will tell him of the family meeting, tonight, and, uh . . ." he hesitates. "I will tell him what I have learned."

Kyung Jae senses that the conversation is complete and he turns toward the path to his house. Young Kim stands and watches his father turn, with his mind still a little numb from the unexpected news. He begins to walk slowly in the direction of Ki Jun's house. But, he walks hesitantly, as if he were walking in the midst of clouds on a mountain crest. Mysteriously, it is like he is in an unfamiliar, enigmatic place, rather than the village in which he has lived, worked and played all his life.

Ki Jun is about to arrive at his house as he returns from the activities of the day. Miss Oh is walking in the opposite direction, toward him. They encounter one another just before he turns to enter his house. He does not invite her into the house unaccompanied, but, they both recognize Young Kim at the same time, coming toward them, a great distance away.

First, Ki Jun says, "Isn't that Young Kim? He walks like a shaman [2]! It is as if he's in a trance! I haven't ever seen him walk in such a peculiar way, like that!" He exclaims, thinking it might be from the earlier numb feeling, "Maybe he has taken the life of the troupe of strolling actors seriously!"

As Young Kim approaches Miss Oh and Ki Jun, he opens the large, wooden gate of the courtyard. Just then, Ki Jun turns and enters his house after asking Miss Oh to excuse him. He clears the room of the few items he had earlier left astray. Still, he keeps his home neat, and he has some carefully chosen simple, but classic items of Korean furniture.

Ki Jun likes neatness, but he does not need to be obsessive in cleaning his house. Still, he quickly does some adjusting here and there in anticipation of two house guests who will enter in a moment. If it seems to be a compulsion to clean house, it is only because it has become another domestic discipline and he enjoys the beauty and comfort of an ordered house.

---

2. *Mudang*

Thus, Ki Jun is very content and satisfied. He enjoys his living conditions. He smiles, also happy to share this little haven with his close friends. He curiously looks quickly outside to see Young Kim walking up the steps as Miss Oh enters. He is patient enough to withhold his own opinions until after he hears Young Kim speak.

"Hello," Young Kim bows and smiles awkwardly at his two friends.

"Hello," they echo, almost in unison.

Young Kim does speak first, and says, "I am sorry, but I have had an unusual experience, and I still feel a little dizzy." He feels the chair to be a solid place to anchor himself after he walked the controlled walk. It was as if he was on a small boat being tossed on great, rolling waves of the sea. "But, I am happy, and I have some great news that I want to share with both of you about plans that our village may soon make."

Please excuse me," Miss Oh interrupts. "I very much want to hear the news, but first I feel a deep need. Young Kim, may we talk for at least just a short while?

"Oh, Ki Jun, this may sound silly and old fashioned, but while we walk the distance from the house, I would like to ask you to do us the favor to just watch, as we go?" Miss Oh asks, seriously. "We would just like to keep ourselves accountable, at all times! Please?"

"Of course," Ki Jun answers. "No problem at all."

"Thank you. Then, Young Kim, will you walk outside with me, that we might talk about something very important?" she asks. "You can have all the time you need to tell us the great news, after we talk. Is that all right, Young Kim?"

"Yes, Miss Oh," Young Kim agrees. "Please excuse us for a few minutes, Ki Jun. We have something to discuss, which is overdue! We will not be long."

Miss Oh's careful request is meant to protect their relationship. Now, the couple will not break with tradition by being together, alone. Especially, as they are attracted to one another, they both know how easily their good intentions can be overcome by temptation.

"I have just heard the news about the accident with the men of the next village, Miss Oh," Young Kim says to her, and he moves closer to her. He wants to speak as carefully as possible. "It was so terrible that I was overcome with emotion, so much. Both my father and I were scarcely able to move or talk for a time, Miss Oh."

"What happened, Young Kim?" Miss Oh asks, as they begin to walk toward the wooded area from which Young Kim had come. "Are you able to tell me, now? Or, do you want to wait?"

Young Kim considers his response. To be with Miss Oh has a sobering effect on Young Kim. It is sobering, partly because of his deeper realization and awareness of her beauty—a simple beauty, without pretense. Now, he feels more alive in the present moment with her, and he wants to let his words to her be 'just right'; neither casual, nor sloppy.

"But, I do not want to confuse you, so I would like to take some time to be certain that I understand how you feel about the Specialized Farmers Music," Miss Oh offers.

"Thank you for your desire to talk about that subject, Miss Oh. I appreciate your concern. It is something about which I have clearly determined in my mind. The news of the next village was an influence to my decision, but I will only speak now about what you have asked.

"Yes, as I told you, I was impressed with what I saw at the farmers music performance in the next village," Young Kim says. "I saw creativity that was free and unrestrained. That appealed to me, very much.

"But, now I can see the same thing with different eyes," Young Kim continues. "Now I see with the eyes of Young Kim the Common-labor Association member, and band member. For, that is who and what I am, in the service of Hananim," he says, adding emphasis to the last words. "Rather than the eyes of Young Kim the self-limiting prisoner, who is anxious to break free and set the world afire." Young Kim's soberness now begins to produce noticeable boldness in his character.

Miss Oh is surprised at this new, philosophical perspective from Young Kim, and she is unsure how to respond.

"Miss Oh, it is only love!" Young Kim exclaims boldly. "The life we live is good. And, how can I do anything except love that which is good, and that which is given to me?" To that, Young Kim adds, "Now, I see myself living as who I am, not living as someone I think I could be. What will I become, simply because it would be what and who I am not?" Is that clear to you; is it logical enough to be understood, Miss Oh?

"Yes, logical," she answers uneasily, as she is unfamiliar with this kind of conversation with Young Kim. "But, if I understand you, you are saying that you see that a change in type of lifestyle is somewhat like a dream that is not realistic? Is that true?"

"Yes, it is true." Young Kim answers, as her close friend. "And by our standards, it is not a responsible action." As they walk, Young Kim becomes silent, turns sensitively and with understanding, and says, "I was not consciously aware until right now, but, real, intimate relating and communication is what my soul thirsts for. Right now, you are giving that to me. It is what I need, and I appreciate that so much!

"May we sit together on that big, flat rock, over there in the warm sunshine, Miss Oh," suggests Young Kim. "Ki Jun can still see us there. We will not spend much time there. Then, we can walk to return to Ki Jun's house. Together, let us wisely use our time, here." Ki Jun walks behind, patiently—at a distance.

Young Kim leads as they walk to the rock. He sits down and moves a little toward Miss Oh after she makes herself comfortable on the large, flat and warm slab of dark, native rock. Having cozied next to each other in the warm sun, they become quickly and warmly comfortable.

Then, Miss Oh speaks, "I was confused that you, being committed to us, even with the potential commitment you have with me—and with your background in this village—that you would forget the values that contribute to strength and true happiness—for each one of us!"

"Thank you for your openness and sincerity, Miss Oh. I appreciate your insights," he answers tenderly. "I did not realize the depth of the process in which I found myself. Truly, I was infatuated with change. And, with novelty," Young Kim says with clarity, which he grasps even as he speaks. "It may have even been an enchantment, which I must now admit I let entrap me."

"What do you mean by 'enchantment'" she echoes his word, asking him with slight mimicry in her voice, clearly meant to be cynical. She then closely studies the look in his eyes[3], hoping to understand what his heart is really saying at the moment.

"I was fascinated; captivated," Young Kim confesses, reflecting upon the prior day. "It was like I had been in a spell, but it did not feel like a spell to me at that time! After I heard the news and I look back at what I had thought and began to do, well . . ." he hesitates. "Yes, I was captivated by *something*!

"Only now, do I more clearly understand what my father has been saying to me, and to Ki Jun." Young Kim still speaks gently, and with passion. "He was really reminding me of the deepest feelings of what he knows are in my own heart, and about his people, and my people. He was explaining about *our* people, Miss Oh! He also explained to me what my heart had forgotten because of life's excitements and 'the fascination of the moment'.

"Yes, for a time I forgot the real object of my life's love, here in this land," Young Kim confesses, "that we would see reunification. I forgot because of the possibilities which lured my thoughts and heart away.

Both Young Kim and Miss Oh become silent, letting his last words reach down and settle within them. Young Kim realizes that by his openness, he makes himself vulnerable with Miss Oh. Nevertheless, he knows that doing *that* is the right thing, and more importantly, that it is necessary for the health of their relationship. He realizes that he has not actually 'confessed' anything serious to her, before this time.

---

3. *kibun*, the eyes are the keys to the being, disclosing a 'right mood' or an 'unacceptable state of being'; i.e. one's *kibun*. It is also the key to how one responds to a person—the premier rule is never to disturb one's kibun!

"What did your father tell you, Young Kim?" asks Miss Oh.

"He reminded me that for me to want to choose to leave the village, the village lifestyle, and the commitment that is part of living here, and to pursue my own personal desires, independent of everybody, and all the intrinsic values of the village . . ." Young Kim looks away and cannot continue, but Miss Oh does it for him.

"That is like what happened when 'the Great Leader' of North Korea, Kim Il Sung chose to leave behind the established unity of our nation. A unity that came at a great cost; a high price," she says.

"He acted independently and militarily against his own people and his own nation. Why? His purpose was to accomplish some idealistic, political results, in order to seek and achieve his own belief system. Is that what you believed?" she asks. "And, does such betrayal always begin with one's turning away from the will of *the Father* [4], *Hananim*?"

Now Young Kim feels free, by way of confession. He turns to face her, and he looks intently into her eyes. "Yes, that is *just* what I was thinking. It is taking the same risks and the same violence of shattering of established relationships. The Communist leader acted on a different scale. In both cases, there would be a rebellion against an established order. And, I am now better able to understand that the more anyone knows God and His Word, the better and easier it will be for him or her to avoid taking a wrong direction, or walking on the wrong path to one's destination.

---

4. *Aboji*

"So, for the reasons just given, I do not think that anyone who joins a Specialized Farmers Band is necessarily being rebellious, but when strong, ancient and intimate relationships are broken to do that—or anything—*then* that is a choice which may often leave suffering victims. Rejection by those who once were near and trusted can bring deep hurt, especially when there are abrupt changes. Such changes are not always to be controlled. Nevertheless, division will often result.

"Reunification," Young Kim says the power-filled *buzz word*, "for Korea, can be seen like letting myself—or anyone—continue to work for the good of every community member. We are taught to sincerely and unconditionally care for all community members.

"*And* the helpless," Young Kim expresses the depths of his heart to Miss Oh. "That is love. How can there be hope or reunification if I turn away, or anybody, turns away from those with whom we live and work, and from those who are also dependent upon us?"

"We cannot, or should not, Young Kim," Miss Oh answers, and Young Kim feels reaffirmed.

"Because you have known me for so many years, you know that reunification is a precious treasure to me," Young Kim says, as he pours forth his passion. "Clearly, most of the people in the nation, or *the entire* nation, cannot be totally whole until the deep wounds are healed. The wounded part, which is left torn apart, is the heart of Korea.

"It is the sum total of every individual's broken heart. It is the people's *han* [5], left as a legacy to follow one with

---

5. *han*, is the Korean term for 'incurable suffering' of the soul; the enduring suffering of the 'Korean national, collective, heart'.

high ideals. This leaving brought a great division to this land, which already had a history of divisions."

"Could it be the birth of the 'new han'; the deep Korean sorrow, which is beyond man's understanding?" asks Miss Oh.

"Except by divine healing, my heart will not be fully healed until I see the hearts of our entire nation healed, Miss Oh," Young Kim says as the expression of his life's great desire.

"Concerning reunification, the torn Korean hearts can only be healed from heaven—healing of hearts which broken by the division of our land cannot be entirely healed even by *a good reunification*," he continues. "Would it not be beyond our imagination to see our nation unified again with an economy made strong by people living as a group; people who take care of one another?

Miss Oh begins to protest, "But Young Kim . . . !"

"I know," he interrupts. He anticipates and follows her thought. "It can only happen by the unifying power of the One who has held this country in unity long ago, before the political and spiritual divisions in the land. Yes. Only the hand of the Great One, the God of our ancestors is powerful enough to restore what no man or army can ever restore. And, it is only by His limitless love that we, His people, can work in a unified and harmonious way to accomplish this labor of love.

"I will do any good thing to see our kinsmen and women living as one people, once again, as before. And, even better than before!" Young Kim promises. "And now, Miss Oh, I see that I cannot just do 'anything'. But, what I must do is . . . 'nothing'. I cannot turn away from doing the good and true things that I have learned since

I was a child. Neither can I turn from my desire to try to accomplish more of what is good and true. I cannot go beyond God in my own desires and my own strength.

"No. I must not turn aside for my own gain and satisfaction." Young Kim's says. It would be just as in our village. There would be equality, and decisions would still be reached via republican-democratic, legislative procedures.

"This is something that must grow by inspiration of the words of our banner, Miss Oh. The people must make profound choices—all across the nation. They must choose between unrestrained socialism, unrestrained capitalism, or the choice of serving others. There may be, for an indefinite time, a balance of freely chosen lifestyles. Then, it is my hope that the people will choose a way that is pleasing to the Divine Giver of the Gift of Farming, Miss Oh.

"People must only become members of the group if they perceive the goodness and rightness of the ways of the volunteer or common-labor association. The way we work is as common-laborers, in volunteer service for the good of all community members," says Young Kim, being filled with as much emotion as Miss Oh can remember.

As Miss Oh sees the depth of Young Kim's commitment, she is stimulated with feelings of genuine hope.

"We have been given a vision of the history of the world," Young Kim says, as a summary of his thoughts. "We have seen that man's ideas, however noble they appear, will not endure without the clear guidance of— and, I must emphasize, and say it again—of *Hananim* the God of our ancestors and our own God.

Young Kim continues, "Of course, for centuries, members of Common-labor associations did not know that the God of Heaven is the One who ultimately, also governs earth, Miss Oh." Young Kim thus expresses his love of Korean history, like his father does. "But, they did know that we have received divine gifts, as we see daily. For, it is written across our big banner which tells the world from where our blessings come. We have learned that He is the One who gave the occupation of farming to our beautiful and productive land. I am very thankful that because of the tradition of knowing *Hananim* and His ways, I have received the inheritance of knowledge of His omnipotence, as well as the delegated authority corrupted and possessed by the devil. And, I am thankful to know of the devil's *temporary* control over the earth. But, only those who would not receive the free gift of the power of God's Spirit, from above, are the one's who are also ultimately controlled by the devil's powers."

"Yes, Young Kim," Miss Oh answers. "But, there is something which I must confess to you before we continue our discussion. It is true that our work and lifestyle would not easily be called Farmers music of a common-labor association without the truth which the banner proclaims. But, in my personal time, you know that I have been getting trained as a nurse. Very soon, I will qualify to practice as a licensed nurse.

"More importantly Young Kim, I've seen a real value that you and I—and most of our entire village has been blind to. That is that we have been boasting about our focus on each individual of our village. Yes, we do love everyone with God's unwavering love. But, even as we talk about the Traveling minstrels and their lack of roots being an unpatriotic or non-traditional practice, Young

Kim, please listen to me; we, as members of the Ture Famers music band are not in *total* obedience to the will of God!"

"What do you mean, Miss Oh. That is a strong charge to make."

"Yes, it is strong. But when I count the souls that enter eternity without Christ every day, I shudder. And I realized that when we commit to stay in Suwon-san, we are not obeying God when He commands us to go to all the ends of the earth and make disciples; to tell every creature of God's wonderful plan of salvation. *That* is what I mean and *that* is where there is room for growth that we cannot imagine. And I have a plan, Young Kim."

"How does this new plan match with things about you and me, and the recent plans of our village, Miss Oh?" asks Young Kim.

"Good question. I am glad you asked. It is really not my plan, but God's plan for me, and hopefully us. Your effort to change your values and leave our village, independently, was not as totally wrong as you might think, Young Kim.

"Young Kim, you know that I have been in training to become a nurse." He nods his assent. "And you know that the level of health in Suwon-san is above average."

"Not just above average, Miss Oh. It is much higher than that!" Young Kim exclaims. "People here are almost never sick."

"Exactly. And because of that, you know that I was less excited about my nurse's training, since I may have to find work in another village, town or even the city and leave everyone here that I love."

"Yes. That is something that I had thought might fit in with traveling with a Specialized Farmers band. I was trying to think of how we could integrate my would-be new lifestyle with your nursing. But, I thought, well, it will just work out."

"Maybe you thought that God brought the Specialized Farmers band close to Suwon-san so you could have more excitement in your life, Young Kim. Did you? Well, you don't really have to answer. But, I strongly believe that God brought them into our midst to show us what we were *not* doing, and should have been doing. He just wanted us to see that some of our values are based on our human tradition, and not on His word."

"Miss Oh. You are so blessed! God shows you things that the entire village is blind to—and we have ben blind for such a long time. It is so good that we came away to talk right now."

"Yes, Young Kim, and it is good that the idea of travel has been a hot topic in our community. I have been praying so much about were I could work when my nurse training is complete. Now I have received an answer from Hananim."

"What did He tell you, Miss Oh?" Young Kim asks.

"He told me that I can use my nursing abilities to serve and travel with a medical outreach team, and even go to the North! Isn't that exciting?"

"Yes. But does that coincide with what we might do if things change in our lives? It is like you want to do what I just wanted to do, but didn't. It just doesn't sound too logical to me."

"Correct. And it didn't sound at all logical to me, either, when I first heard God speak to me. But, God, in His perfect wisdom, told me that He would make you become a new Farmers band member. God wants to *morph you*, Young Kim. He wants you to become half

175

Ture Nongak band leader and half Specialized Farmers band leader. He is opening the door to take you and I on the road together! We will be partners in a music ministry—medical team outreach *together*! We will bring God's healing to the people's bodies *and* to their spirits. We will be tools of God's healing of the entire Korean citizen. And, by His grace, we will serve in the entire Peninsula, Young Kim."

Immediately, a huge smile appears on Young Kim's face. He remains silent, overwhelmed and just cannot think of anything to say. He continues to smile and resists a strong urge to take Miss Oh in his arms and express the deep, deep joy that is growing now within him.

"This changes everything!" Miss Oh almost shouts in Young Kim's ears.

Finally Young Kim is able to talk, and he says, "Yes."

They both laugh together for a long time." I felt so secure with our music and our hearts toward God, Young Kim. Then *this* happened. I'm so happy and blessed. We can pray about this in church and ask the elders to join us in prayer, too!"

"There will be a lot of time to help with the project in the next village. It is good that your nurse's training is almost, but not yet complete," Young Kim says, still in a dreamlike state.

"It is good that we have this opportunity to talk, now, Miss Oh," Young Kim's says. "Now, let's go and I will tell Ki Jun our news.

"It would be good to have more times of talking together like this, Miss Oh," Young Kim says.

Spontaneously, he reaches and gently places his hand on Miss Oh's shoulder. With feminine, intuitive sensitivity, she simply says, "Yes," also spontaneously, and recalls their mutual hope and years-old dream.

Her response is no less vague and no less understood than Young Kim's unplanned 'formal' proposal that had no previous form but that of a dream. Then, easily, they both move in unison, rising as if to a light melody, and begin to return to Ki Jun's house.

Young Kim is so encouraged by this meeting!

CHAPTER XI

ONE SOURCE, TWO LIVES, THREE MEN

Neither Young Kim nor Miss Oh is aware that Ki Jun also has something explosive and powerful to tell them, just as they have for him.

Still, Ki Jun waits patiently. For, he thinks his message would have more impact if he lets Young Kim speak first, as previously planned.

"Ki Jun, there are two things I have to tell you," Young Kim says, taking much care to talk calmly. However, the house is filled with an atmosphere of excitement. "The two things are both very serious, and both are related to one another in their effect upon us. Calm yourself, because I do not want to upset you with any of our news. Please do not get upset with me, either, as I share with you what I have chosen as the better of two very attractive opportunities.

"Ki Jun, we have been close friends for many years, and we have played this music and danced the farmers dance on these roads for many years, also. Your friendship is so valuable to me. I would do almost anything to avoid offending you."

"Please feel at peace, Young Kim," Ki Jun responds to comfort Young Kim. "I believe you will be happy to hear what I have to tell you after you have completed telling your news to me. Please proceed."

"Thank you. I will tell this story to you just as it happened to me," Young Kim says, to begin the story as he shifts his legs under him for more comfort. He wants to get very comfortable to concentrate more fully on what he knows will probably be a long talk.

"Do you remember that they took those two men to the hospital after the car accident on the road to Suwon-san? I am very sad to say that the hospital reports that both men were critically injured in the accident. They are still in critical condition. The doctors are not certain if the men will live!"

"No!" Ki Jun gasps. "I am sorry." He quickly averts his eyes to the ground by his feet. He remains motionless for a while. Silence now becomes the bond between the three.

"The two men have three children who have already lost their mothers!" Young Kim exclaims, himself still unable to believe the degree of difficulty which those children are facing. "Now, there are three more children in their village who could be without mother *and* father. To know about this news makes me very sad."

To have to repeat this news brings a lump to Young Kim's throat, and his eyes become misty. The exhilaration from the preceding time alone with Miss Oh has now been dampened by recalling the tragic news.

"The next village now has so many orphans, Ki Jun," Young Kim says. "What a heavy load it must be for the people just to live in an environment like that." Miss Oh silently nods her agreement. Ki Jun is also silent, too stunned to speak. He had plans to tell his own exciting story which he had formed in his mind. But, when he hears the news that Young Kim just shared, the level of excitement seems to quickly slip away. Now, his news won't have the powerful impact which, just minutes before, he thought it would have had.

"It is not as easy now to share what I have to say, as it would have been before you told me the report about the next village," Ki Jun says, as his sadness becomes apparent. "But, still I have great news. The lead dancer of the specialized farmers band that performed at the next village became very sick, and . . ." Ki Jun hesitates. He is unable to complete his thought, and to ease the awkward stress for Ki Jun, Miss Oh conveniently interrupts him.

"Excuse me, Ki Jun, Young Kim has not yet told you the second part of his story. Please listen and he will finish telling the story."

"Okay. Please excuse me, but I was so excited about my own news, that I forgot that Young Kim has more to tell," Ki Jun apologizes. His communication is not very convincing. Still, he will not do anything but reveal his focus on the new music and performance that has come to town.

Then, without hesitating, Young Kim continues. "It is not a coincidence that these events happened at the same time, Ki Jun. So, I must tell this very important news, also. I consider it important, especially now, because it affects each one of us. Because of the unexpected accident, there are more children without parental protection in that village. That is a simple fact that we are all aware of. Sadly, there were very many children like that, already.

"Significantly, before the accident, there were negotiations about our association doing some benefit work in the next village. You must have been too busy to have heard the news. But, the benefit work will facilitate us to teach them by modeling the Volunteer-labor lifestyle.

"My father explained to me that we must all agree to be willing to take this responsibility, or we cannot accept the task," Young Kim continues.

"Most important, is the fact that there is now a real need of laborers in that village. The harvest is near, and yet many men are not able to work. And, of course, there are those young children without parents who have nobody to provide for, or care for them. Therefore, we are presented with a choice to help them, or decide not to. It is really a simple choice."

"This is such an unexpected and abrupt situation, Young Kim. Who could have expected this? It is so difficult. How can I decide?" asks Ki Jun.

"Let me tell you how I decided, Ki Jun," Young Kim offers to explain. "Because I was . . . I mean, you know we were . . . so excited to see the performance of the troupe of strolling actors—that I lost touch with our commitment of accountability to the community. At that time, I realized that according to our Ture social code, you and I cannot make independent decisions to leave our community responsibilities."

"Cannot?" Ki Jun protests.

"How could we have ignored that integral part of the essence of the very life of our community, here?" answers Young Kim. "It is something unthinkable."

Ki Jun listens, thinks a moment, hesitates and responds. "It is difficult to admit, but you are right, Young Kim. I do not know how we, or anybody, could forget or reject such a basic principle of our community commitment as that.

"Yet now, Young Kim, I see that you and I did just that. And, I would join you in quickly revising my thinking to accept the right choice to help the needy families and orphans of Suwon-san and the next village. But . . ." Ki Jun hesitates at this point. He feels an awkward moment, not knowing just what to say, or how to say it.

Young Kim speaks, "My father is calling an emergency meeting of *the Common-labor group* [1] leaders to get a consensus of opinion about this matter. It would mean more work for everybody. It is not a decision to be made lightly, or without much consideration."

"That is true, Young Kim," Ki Jun quickly answers. "Now, I will tell you my news. Uh," he hesitates, "well, as I began to say earlier, the *specialized farmers music and* dance [2] team, that we saw perform, has left the next village and they are going to a place in the province of Ch'ungch'ongnam-do, to the south.

"Their lead dancer is very sick, Young Kim," Ki Jun says, now with both excitement and disappointment in

---

1. *ture/doorae.*
2. *namsadang p'ae.*

his voice. "And," Ki Jun now chooses his words carefully, "they knew that I had the ability and experience for some of the same farmers music and dance that they perform. They asked me if I could help them, Young Kim!

"It is only temporary, until their lead dancer recovers," he adds.

"Young Kim, I told them that I would help them in this time of need. They have a performance scheduled for two days from now."

At that moment, Miss Oh returns to the room with a tray of hot tea. She stops, bends down and sets the tray on the low, black-lacquered table which stands between them. Her arrival is perfectly timed to relieve the tension which has been increasing between the two young men—two young men who have been close friends for so many years.

Miss Oh says simply, "Shall we take time from the conversation to gather our thoughts and enjoy one another's presence! There is so much good news to share!"

The three all smile, and the two men nod their agreement simultaneously. Although Young Kim has sucked in his breath upon hearing Ki Jun's report, he still withholds blurting out a groan of surprise, and mixed emotion. Still, he silently takes the hot tea that Miss Oh serves him. Then, together, as they savor the taste of the warming drink, each quietly and reflectively begins to contemplate life's unexpected surprises.

Miss Oh knows that Young Kim has deep feelings within him, and she wants to speak boldly. Young Kim, too, feels much like a simmering volcano, ready to erupt within.

Still feeling bold confidence, Miss Oh, announces to the two band members that despite that the Co-operative-labor leaders' meeting had not yet decided about the work in the next village. And, although Young Kim and she had not decided what the results of that decision would mean, importantly, Ki Jun must understand that the present time is very critical for everyone in both Suwon-san, and the next village, and especially for she and Young Kim.

The two men silently think about her words, for a time. Young Kim stifles a smile—with much difficulty.

Ki Jun then announces, "Yes, Miss Oh, I know that the importance of this time is very great to our villages, more than anything else that I had considered, or even dreamed it would be."

Before he can continue, Miss Oh says, "Then, we must not lose any time. We cannot even think of the offense that somebody would certainly bring if they were to leave the Volunteer-labor community without having first the approval of the family group, or the Association members.

"That would be so offensive! Nobody would ever do that!" Miss Oh exclaims. "Oh, Ki Jun, you must have been so infatuated and intrigued with the specialized farmers music performance, just like Young Kim!"

"Yes!" The two chime in unison. "We were," they say, completing the thought, this time not quite synchronized. Then, they quickly give one another embarrassed glances.

Despite feeling very awkward as a Korean woman to have uncharacteristically embarrassed the two men, Miss Oh is now energized, and continues, "I am sorry! Please forgive me. I must tell you about tomorrow. My cousin the teacher, and some others and I are going to the next village to visit the school. Would you please accompany us, that we all might have a firsthand experience of that village?

"I believe that it would help you see more clearly, if you need to ask for a group decision about farmers music. Or, it could help you if you would be interested in serving in another village besides our own. I think that the leaders will tell us that we will benefit in many years, by helping those orphans-and by helping the farmers, too!" Almost out of breath, Miss Oh completes her thought.

"Thank you for the offer, Miss Oh," Ki Jun says. "I do not know, at this moment, how to decide, since I realize that my earlier decision about farmers music is a decision made without sufficient consideration.

"Yes!" Ki Jun speaks abruptly. "I do think that this is the way to let you and your friends rescue me. Sure, I would like very much to go with you and your friends, tomorrow. It should help me gain perspective in my choices."

Ki Jun stands, and steps into the kitchen area. There, he finds a plastic bag on the shelf, filled with one of his favorite foods. When he returns to the table, he pours a small mound of dried squid slivers onto a plate. There is enough for all three of them to enjoy the tasty, Korean specialty.

He then returns to the food area and places some pickled radish and cabbage[3] in small bowls. His two guests, however, do not have appetites, in light of the afternoon's events. Both Young Kim and Miss Oh's minds are deeply concerned and occupied about the newfound responsibilities of the day. And, they are being

---

3. *kimchee*

touched in their own hearts by their personal talk before returning to Ki Jun's home.

The couple realizes they are beginning to experience more unity in their thoughts and their shared goals. They both now know that something meaningful is happening, although not fully realized.

Miss Oh and Young Kim make arrangements for the morning, after they each take only a few small slivers of dried seafood which Ki Jun offers to them. They each just want something in their stomach, so that hunger pangs will not distract them from their common goal.

They are restless, so the couple stands and begins to stretch their legs. Their minds shift from the moment to tomorrow's responsibilities. Miss Oh blurts out, "Ki Jun, I will soon work as a nurse, and I am prepared to travel to many villages with Young Kim's farmers band!"

Ki Jun doesn't quite follow Miss Oh's thought. He answers, "Is Young Kim now in the Namsadang p'ae, or has the Ture nongak taken on a new identity? I don't understand."

"We have plans to change our lifestyles, radically — and all because of a revelation of God's true will for us and the band, Ki Jun. We will explain more, later.

"My friends want to leave for the next village as soon as possible, when they learn of the decision of the village elder/leaders' meeting," Miss Oh says, and she expects to see Ki Jun early the next morning, soon after the sun fully rises above the horizon and the mountain.

The couple then moves toward the door, and as they do, Ki Jun notices that they are walking in unison — as if on a morning drill, marching and dancing in the farmers band — or, like an ancient, musical, military, quasi-militia, 'alert team'! Ki Jun chuckles to himself.

Though he sees them take only a few steps, Ki Jun also notices that the two walk more closely than ever, and very naturally, too!

He smiles within, and politely withholds any indication of betraying his thought to his 'newly reunited' friends. He does not know what happened to these two, but now he perceives that he is witnessing a literal blossoming. This, Ki Jun feels very deeply in his heart, is the blossoming of a true and lasting love. With all his heart he hopes that it will truly be both true and lasting.

CHAPTER XII

THE CHALLENGE OF THE SUWON-SAN LIFESTYLE

K i Jun is well rewarded for his roles as a worker and as the music and dance band leader. He knows his responsibilities. As he receives authority to do his job, he is confident—and he does his job, and does it well, indeed. He really has very little knowledge of the neighboring village, however, and the dynamics of how it and Suwon-san differ. For that reason, he feels that he needs to be at his best for the outing with the group.

He also wants to compensate for the embarrassment of the events of the prior day. So, he prepares for a positive response from Miss Oh and her group. Before he goes to sleep he anticipates the next day's outing. He carefully lays out his clothes and his backpack to be well prepared for the next day at the village. He and others now dub the village as the 'orphan village'. If he does not awake before the group comes to his house, he knows that he can still prepare quickly to be ready.

"My mind is alert for tomorrow morning,' he tells himself. "I will be able to listen for any sound that may notify me as the group approaches the house.' He knows that when he hears the cadence of the feet on the dirt path and the faint sound of joyful singing, that he will be ready to rise up from sleep and quickly prepare himself.

'*I* will rise quickly, put on the traditional white clothes of the peasant and reach the door before *the group* reaches my door. They will not need to wait for me,' he assures himself. 'I will be ready to join this group for the adventure to our neighbor village.

Soon, the sounds of heavenly voices are in Ki Jun's ears. He sleeps deeply all night, accompanied by some extensive, dramatic dreams.

As the sweet melody continues, he soon awakens and recognizes the singing tones of Miss Oh and the mother of Young Kim. As planned, he quickly dresses himself, and dashes through the doorway with his pack clutched firmly in his hand. Just then, the group turns along the curve in the path, and comes into view as they approach the house. As the group moves near to the house, they sing the women's chorus.

When the group is just a few steps away, Ki Jun demonstrates his value of group unity. He jumps in—in time with the cadence of the group's ongoing dance-march, without causing the need for anyone to pause, nor lose their marching cadence. Everyone smiles.

The singing continues joyously and vigorously as the excited group moves along next to widely-spaced, parallel rows of tall, wind-break trees. The trees are acoustic sentinels, which reflect the singing—by both reflecting and sending the life-filled sounds skyward.

Quickly, Ki Jun is invigorated with the adrenaline of the abrupt post-sleep action and sudden physical exhilaration of group dancing and singing. He proceeds with the group along the path, moving in unity with rhythmic cadence.

'Mostly women comprise this group,' Ki Jun thinks to himself as he notices the elevated tonal quality of the song they sing. 'I am very happy that the women are very enthused, now,' he thinks to himself. 'This is a great way to begin a day.' The women are truly happy. It is like they are going to a big, annual celebration.

But, he now notices an unstable feeling within, but he does not know why. He reflects, 'I feel very satisfied with the concern of our village. I am thankful also for the concern which is shown me by village members. There is a sense of a loss of freedom which I do not understand. 'Too much thought,' he finally suggests to himself. 'I must forget myself and concentrate on being a reliable member of this group of ambassadors-of-fellowship to our neighbors.

As Ki Jun marches forward on the path, he recalls his community responsibilities—and how that contrasts with his earlier desire to leave his village to gain membership in the specialized farmers music band. If and when he did leave, it would be treading this very path, even as he is now doing.

'Except,' he thinks, 'the radical difference is that I would be moving with my back to the group.' Yes. He would be moving *away* from the group, *and* away from the cause of this group of ambassadors.

To his relief, and to fulfill an immediate need, Ki Jun lets himself be swept away. He is totally swept away by exhilaration and by his integration with the group's unified excitement and zeal[1]. The enthusiasm[1] and joy is irresistible. He catches himself beginning to sing all the women's songs. He would rather contribute to the group's solidarity as a unified group, than to isolate himself with self-conscious embarrassment and reduce overall unity.

Instead, though his heart has been captured by an opportunity to 'escape', which recently tempted and overcame him, he still revels in the full sense of belonging to and identifying with this marching, dancing, singing and celebrating group. For him, it is an experience of a wide chasm, a great distance from the usual, routine of life, about which his mind had been deceived, telling him that it would be boring.

The women do not pay special attention to his singing, but all continue with unified exuberance. Everyone sings—excellently and wholeheartedly! The group sings of a new day of opportunity, of their hopes for a prosperous day on the earth, and for the soil, which is a part of their heavenly inheritance.

The cheerful group continues to march and dance along the path. The group sings from their hearts,

---

1. *heung*, (enthusiasm.)

believing that the heavy burdens of the village they are approaching will begin to be lightened. They sing forth the message of hope that even their neighbors can sense—that help is on the way! Great hope feeds their zeal and their zeal feeds their faith! Now, Ki Jun is ecstatic! His whole being explodes in a steady stream of rejoicing!

The group enthusiastically begins to sing an accompanying chorus to the song they have been singing, just as they enter the border of the thatch-roofed village houses. They complete the chorus just as they come to rest in a small, clear, grassy area away from the houses. Miss Oh, her cousin and her mother all turn to Ki Jun and begin to tell him the day's agenda.

As they approach, Ki Jun turns to greet the older women with deep, respectful bows. Then, he greets the women warmly. "Thank you for inviting me to join this group, today," he says. "I must be bold to say to you that it is both rare and unusual that I, a man, would be invited to dance and sing in a group of women." He thinks that under ordinary circumstances he would be embarrassed. But he says, "Although it is uncommon that there are only women in this group, I consider it a privilege and an honor. Why? Because, it is an opportunity to serve the people of this village, as a team."

This is Ki Jun's declaration, meaning that the group is important; and that traditional values may be important, but they must not block God's commission for giving honor to the farmers' vocation, with all of the ramifications that support Godly principles.

Ki Jun steps boldly now toward Miss Oh. He leans near her and almost whispers in her ear. Then, he says, "Shall we go ahead of the others, together, that we might accomplish our task?" Ki Jun believes that this will earn him more respect in the group, and that he will be noticed by Miss Oh.

Surprised by Ki Jun's actions, Miss Oh steps back, and says, "Yes. We have been asked as a group to speak to some people at the school. Can we still meet them if we are not together with the group? I do not see how that will be possible, Ki Jun." Miss Oh answers her own rhetorical question as politely as the moment allows.

But, Ki Jun ignores the answer. Instead, he brings his face close to hers, and persists. He says, "Miss Oh, I respect you very much. I truly want to tell you how much you mean to me. Your influence upon me has been a stabilizing force, and I value that, very highly." Both he and Miss Oh know that he is now beyond proper protocol.

"Can't we walk just a little behind the others as we go to the school?" he questions. "There is so much that you could tell me about this place. This time, Miss Oh totally ignores *him*. She turns to the group to make the announcement, "Let's all go together to the school."

"We are very excited about giving this gift," Young Kim's mother quickly adds, with great enthusiasm.

Miss Oh's cousin, Chun Ja, expresses her confirmation about the gift. She says, "I have not seen a group as committed to doing good things for people of another village — as you and this group. Your volunteer-labor group has astounded me these few days of my visit, whenever I have seen them.

"Yes. I am impressed. I am even more impressed that you saw in me a capacity which I did not know existed. Thank you, so much."

Interrupting, Ki Jun asks, "Which is that?"

"You must wait until we reach the school to learn the answer, Ki Jun," answers Dan Bae. "The gift is a special surprise to all, and we cannot reveal it to anybody until the time of its presentation. Then everybody will be surprised. Even you will be!" With this, Ki Jun again moves closer to Miss Oh. Again, he leans close, and without shame, he whispers, "You can tell me what the surprise is. And, even if you will not tell, it is O.K, for I want to help you today, in any way I can."

Though Miss Oh sees Ki Jun as being forward, nevertheless, she is surprised by his persistence. She decides not to answer him, and remains silent.

The group turns with the road to walk between widely spaced farmhouses that have adjacent plots of farmland behind. As the group proceeds, and as they approach the center of the village, the farmhouses are spaced a little closer together. The center-most houses are owned by those merchants and tradesmen who do not actually do farm work.

Ki Jun uses the more concentrated spacing of the houses as a clue to intensify his challenge to Miss Oh. Thus, he concentrates his effort to gain Miss Oh's confidence. "I have decided to try to do anything that I am able, that I might serve this village with the Common-labor group[2] , Miss Oh," Ki Jun says in a serious tone. Miss Oh's raises her eyebrows slightly as she now detects a little drama in his voice, of which she was not previously aware.

Ki Jun speaks to test Miss Oh to learn if she wants to care for the alone and frightened children, here. "Ki Jun,

2. Ture

please remember that there are many such children here, and the need is also great. The school may offer us many opportunities."

Ki Jun wants to make a point before arriving at the school, so he quickly asks, "Do you think there may be a position of responsibility for me to take, available at the school? I mean, like what you just mentioned. It may present a challenge to do *common-labor Farmers music and dance* [3] here, as well as take a position at the school. So, I do want to be available to help you." After saying this, Ki Jun thinks his persistence is hot! As hot, he thinks, as the hottest, spiciest *kimchee* [4] he has ever eaten! 'That is hot *kimchee*!' he thinks. Ki Jun sometimes feels compelled to motivate himself in such a manner.

Again, Miss Oh does not respond to Ki Jun's challenge. Neither does she know how to answer him, nor just what is his purpose. The silence brings a tension between them.

Unexpectedly, Young Kim's mother and Chun Ja begin to sing a schoolchildren's song, in harmony. They sing in playful and childlike tones and began to skip like playful children. As the group walks along, they soon see the schoolyard filled with children. They notice that the children are not moving about in play, or laughing and shouting, as schoolchildren typically do.

The women skip and sing loudly in an effort to inspire any child who may notice them, and to 'let themselves go' to help facilitate their arrival for the children. They know that this is an action involving risk, but they love the joy it brings to them. The two women are aware that

3. *Ture/doorae nongak*
4. Marinated and spiced cabbage and turnips—a Korean staple.

they are on a mission of bringing and restoring joy to this little village. So, they think that there is not a better time than now to act upon that conviction.

In any event, the women know of the priceless value of love sent from The One who, millennia ago, commissioned their work.

As they draw closer to the school, almost each member of the group now realizes that 'the burden of proof' is now theirs. They must prove that the 'Great, Eternal life force is immeasurably greater than the ideal of the *self-reliance*, [5] of the North. Knowing that this key-word would be found constantly on the lips of those of the Communist regime in the North, it is also an effective device to capture young minds in the North, the young counterparts of these schoolchildren, here. Miss Oh thinks to herself, 'Like the strong ox that threshes or plows, if it falls into the canal, there is no way it can be self-reliant. The owner must come and pull it from the water—to save its life. Many times, people too are like the ox.' Thus, Miss Oh reasons to herself.

Her thinking elaborates, 'Yes. People have their own 'canals' into which they can fall, just like the ox. All over the world, people are falling into canals when they think they are very strong.' Miss Oh cannot imagine how she has lived without the help of someone to pull her from certain death. 'We are the ones who have come here to pull these who need help from the 'canal', just like the owner of the ox who pulls his animal from an impossible circumstance.

---

5. *juche,* is the 'salvation motto' of the regime of the North, meaning 'self reliance'.

Ki Jun observes, and vocalizes, "This village is so quiet," speaking directly and only to Miss Oh. "It would be good for the band and I to come and make lively music to help the people here to be happy."

Miss Oh continues her long-held silence. Her thoughts are on the children and their school. She cannot remember seeing anything like what she now sees. As she watches, the children stand almost motionless in the schoolyard. And, she wonders as the children are also almost totally silent.

'They look almost like statues,' she thinks to herself. She sees that the children seem as if there is a dark cloud that hovers over them and has total control over them. She doesn't want to discourage the children so she holds back her tears.

Typically, the children are always busily moving and running around the play area, while raising a loud buzz of excited shouts across the school grounds. These children are not typical children; not today.

"There is so much we can do for these children," Miss Oh says, firmly and resolutely.

Ki Jun continues in his obsession and now attempts another distraction of Miss Oh's thoughts, and says, "Again, Miss Oh, let us not be overly distracted by the problems at this school. We must remember the power of the Common-labor Farmers music, and how we can be servants to everybody.

"Can we go directly to the village elders?" Ki Jun inquires.

Miss Oh feels the time is right to answer, now. "Ki Jun, I am not able to make an independent decision about this." She explains patiently, although she is becoming frustrated.

Miss Oh realizes a parallel between Ki Jun's 'attachment-infatuation' here and his interest in the Specialized Farmers Music show. So, she says to him, "Please be reminded of our Volunteer-labor heritage. We all have a binding agreement to make group decisions, in civic affairs. We are always responsible for every member of the community, Ki Jun. There are few exceptions.

"Young Kim's mother is responsible for this time of investigation, here," Miss Oh explains. "You could ask *her*—if you wish to continue to pursue your ideas."

Ki Jun and the rest of the group are startled when they hear the softly spoken, "Hello, Good morning," by an elderly, white-haired woman, who smiles and humbly bows deeply. "We are so happy and thankful that you came to our little village from Suwon-san. Will you please come to be with some of our children? They would be very excited to meet neighbors from your village. Come."

"Thank you, very much, Mrs. Choi," Miss Oh answers. "It is our pleasure to have the opportunity to come here. How could we refuse to come and give you aid after a tragic occurrence has happened to the people of your village? We've come to help you with all of your needs. We also would like to share our talents and skills with the any member of this village."

"In Suwon-san, we find joy, peace, and commitment. Hananim has blessed our village with prosperity since we live as a community with the volunteer-labor lifestyle," Miss Oh continues. "We enjoy this, almost without exception. More importantly, we know that we can, and must, give and share those talents that are so marvelously bestowed upon us. Yes, we know that it is another divine gift. And, we are thankful that our Source is pleased to have the ability to make those talents even greater. We learn that as we let go of our gifts, He gives them back to us, with more added, Mrs. Choi!"

"We have heard some things about your village," Mrs. Choi responds, in a complimentary way. "You know how the people talk. When people from your village live differently than others, we know that what we hear about them can change from ear to ear and mouth to mouth.

"We all know the Korean proverb, don't we, 'that the beginning and the end are the same'? Mrs. Choi asks. "Your dependability will be proven in the end, just as it has been seen from the start. We will see what will happen, and I think that your dependability will be seen through your work, no matter if it is in Suwon-san, or outside of Suwon-san.

"I must tell you about our school. The children are becoming discouraged. Each time there is a misfortune, or if a child loses his or her father or mother, it seems as if these children are affected so deeply. Well, as you can see here, since the other day when the accident happened, the children are very sensitive to the loss of their classmates.

"Our school was less active than the other schools in the area. And, as you can see now, it is so inactive that it seems to be like a place that the children have come to—to do nothing. It looks like the children are waiting for something special to happen. It is almost like they are waiting to come to life!" Mrs. Choi chokes back her tears. "We are so thankful that you to have come to our village to help us. You are needed here. These little ones need you, even more.

Mrs. Choi's words touch the hearts of each member of the group. Miss Oh is especially touched by what Mrs.

Choi says and begins to be choked with emotion, too. She is surprised that she is able to resist tears, as she sees or feels a clearly tragic problem. Still, she now finds it difficult to swallow.

She sees the vulnerability of these precious little ones who are so dependent on more mature and responsible people than themselves. This actually speaks to her very being; which brings a momentary pause to her normal daily activity.

Miss Oh is affected when she sees the children, and, as she is remembering the village's condition, she can barely speak. Then, with tender emotion, she says, "Mrs. Choi, we are really thankful for the opportunity to be here in your village. The volunteer labor form of work is for the good of *each person* in the community, without exception. We still respect that parents are the primary protectors of children. We believe *that* is the rule from heaven. Another duty is that the weak and needy are cared for: and, of course, children are always important to us.

As the group begins to walk again, the women talk to the children. The perimeter of the schoolyard is the path preferred by Mrs. Choi. That path is adjacent to large, flourishing, green shade trees. The beautiful trees enhance the walk-and-talk for all.

Young Kim's mother nods her head to Miss Oh to continue to speak, to give her authority to do so.

After she takes two or three steps, Miss Oh stops and kneels down to the children's eye level, and says "The men work in the field so much, and sometimes, as is usual, the women will work with them in times of need. Otherwise, the women have other responsibilities, like your mothers have, and the other women, here. We are here to be with you and we will help you.

Then, Miss Oh stands to continue her conversation with Mrs. Choi. She begins, "One very important responsibility is to teach the right way to our children. We want them to be educated in the things that will make them responsible citizens and responsible members of the community. We also have a strong desire to see our people with hearts that are happy—especially while they are working so hard every day. That is a great part of why we have come here to share our lives with you.

"As you have heard, our life of volunteer-labor is to work, by consensus, for the welfare of the entire village. The work is to implement ethical principals from the Son of the Great One. To live this way is like taking a journey home from a distant land.

"Each step closer to home brings us more into 'the unseen protection'. That may sound mysterious, but it becomes a daily reality with constant use! Our labor, our happiness and we, ourselves, are fulfilled through letting go of our strong desire to have and constantly increase our own possessions. We must be thankful for all things, so we are thankful to the God of Heaven, *Hananim*. This is how we will serve you.

"Thank you so much, Miss Oh," Mrs. Choi begins. "It is clear that you speak not of your own ideas, but those of your entire village. The children will understand that. In the school here in our village, we have a heavy load."

To emphasize a point Mrs. Choi stops, and the group stops with her. They listen closely as she speaks. "There is a shortage of men to accomplish the farm work, and some women have taken on other responsibilities. And now we do not have enough experienced, trained teachers for our schools. Therefore, we are open and receptive to your offer of all that you are willing to do to help."

Suddenly, the group is interrupted by a group of three young boys who run by the school grounds, screaming loudly. They shout as they run, "Mrs. Choi, Mrs. Choi, you are a teacher of monkeys! Let them out of their cage." With this, they continue to run away, laughing, and they stoop down to pick up little clods of dirt, stand up, and throw them at the group of children.

Surprised, Mrs. Choi pauses to take a deep breath. Then she speaks lowly and softly "It is a little difficult now, but I did begin to say that we too, are now at a time where we must start to be thankful for all that we have, and all that we get. We do have some very great needs.

"Those boys are another example of our great need, here." Just then, the entire group turns at the sound of another clamorous noise of shouting children running toward the group. The playground supervisor has instructed the children to run and shout. With an alert mind and quick thinking, Young Kim's mother immediately responds. She asks Mrs. Choi if they can begin to sing a children's song.

Mrs. Choi quickly nods her assent, and Chun Ja excitedly begins to sing, solo at first. Then, after a few moments, Ki Jun joins her.

Soon, all the women are singing a harmonious echo of an account of what wonderful creatures—what gifts— that children are. They sing directly to the group of children running toward them.

The children arrive with wide smiles and teeth gleaming. At this, each member of the group leans down to pick up a child. They each lift the little ones, and the joy multiplies as each sees another child swing in the air and sees the joy and wonder on the face of each child—who is a recipient of the 'free ride'. Each adult mimics the 'free swing', thus letting the area resemble a small carnival ride. Children swing in all directions.

A group of children wait their turn to fly in circles in the loving arms of a grown-up. They soon get their turn. The playground welcome is complete! Smiles are now on every face, and in each heart! A true bond has been made at the primary school. Happily, the children skip and dance in the play area. In the eyes of Miss Oh, they seem like tiny Farmers band members without instruments, dancing with all their might.

Young Kim's mother asks Mrs. Choi if she can do a special favor for them. The group now wants to pray for the children's well being. Mrs. Choi happily agrees. A circle is formed, and Young Kim's mother softly speaks, "Oh, God of Heaven, our Father, thank you for your immeasurable love. Please show it to these children, more than they have ever seen or experienced before. Thank you, our Lord and God of yesterday, today, and forever."

Peace and calm falls on the group like morning light on the mountain. Not a sound came from anyone's lips, but each person sensed that the others felt the same in his or her heart.

As the adults pass into the school to plan activities, Ki Jun gets Miss Oh's attention. He excuses himself, and then begins to genuinely ask, this time, for forgiveness for his earlier presumptive and manipulative words.

Ki Jun is very embarrassed, and he begins to explain himself. "I see that I formed an attitude against you, Miss Oh. I was spared from further shame by our arrival here at the school, though it was earlier than expected. I actually wanted to say that you are like a North Korean! Yes.

"I cannot believe that I could be like that—or even think like that. I saw you as a naive and unrealistic person in ideas and actions. And, that I was here at the opportune moment to take necessary action," Ki Jun confesses, both embarrassed and relieved. He held a political opinion—a thought—that anybody who can be so dedicated to a *single purpose* must be like a dictator or a Communist country's government agent, with a narrow mind. "I thought of you like one who would spare no life to accomplish your goals. I was so wrong, so wrong!" Ki Jun exclaims.

"Now I see that my thoughts were very ridiculous," Ki Jun says, feeling deep emotion. "My thoughts were selfish, not yours. I must ask you to forgive those hurtful words, which I have spoken—all of them. *It is I* who needs to re-align my thoughts. I have seen now, how a spontaneous gift can be its own reward to both the receiver *and* to the giver! I had been putting *my* values of the worth on my abilities and the role that I had been assigned. It is only by the grace of God that I am able to see my own weaknesses. Now, I am able to respect you more since I can now respect myself."

With that, the two-village meeting time arrives. The agenda is set; to discuss and plan the integration and sharing of some of the workload of the farmland of this village. The agenda includes identifying the responsibilities of the Common-labor group from Suwon-san and the apprenticeship/training of willing workers. All workers who are willing will become candidates for membership for the initial phase of the new, independent Common-labor group. It will be *their* village group. That possibility will depend upon the village elders' decisions.

CHAPTER XIII

WOMEN'S NATIONAL CONTRIBUTION — THE DEFENSE OF LIFE

The schoolteachers of the two villages soon find that they share many common goals and values. They feel very much in accord with one another.

As the agenda of the conference of the representatives of the two villages is fulfilled, Young Kim's mother suggests that the meeting be adjourned and that the group begins the short walk to the elder's home. Miss Oh has made plans with one of the teachers to stay at the school. Together with the schoolgirls, they plan to give a demonstration of a much-loved historical event on the hillside, with singing and dancing. They are planning to teach songs of the traditional, patriotic, women's folk-dance called *Kanggangsull'ae*. This patriotic, Korean dance is performed and danced as a re-enactment of staged military supply troops on a hill near the site of an historic sea invasion.

"We will sing together. It is for girls and women only!" Miss Oh instructs the girls, who are being asked to assemble in a large circle. "Your teacher, Young Kim's mother, and I will sing one verse. Then we will all sing that line together. It will be easy. Let us begin."

Just as if they had rehearsed it well, they all begin to freely dance around the form of a circle, according to tradition. They weave themselves gracefully in and out, as if they were practiced professionals. With harmony, they persist to weave themselves back and forth, through inner and outer circles, moving in opposite directions. The women and girls dance and sing until some start to become tired. But, they do not grow tired very soon, since the excitement gives them more and more energy. However, the girls play so vigorously, and they are excited by this unique *own-gender* work of dance-art.

"We will sing and dance like this again, girls, until you know the dance and the songs well," Miss Oh encourages them. She is quite happy with their enthusiastic response.

"This celebration of songs in this group can help free each of us from fear, just as it did for the women who danced and sang around the big bonfires hundreds of years ago," Young Kim's mother offers.

"The fear which we feel but can't see is being chased away. It is chased by the goodness and strength of the Great One who lives here in our hearts, where He is pleased to be. The fear is chased away now, just as the naval attackers were chased away by the patriotic women simulating fighting troops, on the hillside long ago.

"Each girl hopes gladly for the next chance to dance in the traditional time of women's singing and dancing. Each one has a special desire in her heart to assemble together once again with the others, in this manner, to celebrate their heritage of heroism."

Two young orphan boys who were with the boy's music group across the school play-area, now come to Young Kim's mother to ask her about the music. "Young Kim's mother," Hong Won inquired, "we would like to know about the Farmers music band members, Ki Jun and your son, Young Kim."

"What would you like to know about them, Hong Won? Ask me, and I will tell you," she offers.

"We would like to know if they will be in their Farmers music band for a long time, or if they will join in another farmers music group. You know, like the kind that travels all over the place, doing everything?" Hong Won naively asks.

With this, Chong Won begins to mimic a farmers band member, marching around and pretending to beat both drumheads of the big, *Korean hourglass-shaped drum.*[1] Then he leans way back to hold the imagined drum upright, dramatizing the bulk and weight of the imagined instrument.

The boys giggle slightly, hoping not to lose their serious demeanor of interest. Young Kim's mother looks closely at Hong Won, and explains,

"Those two Common-labor Farmers music band members have made a choice to live a lifestyle to work with and for one-another, in our village. They were recently reminded that they are a part of our village, and they are as important as any other person in the village. We need them so badly, and they will not leave our village, unless most of the people say that they should not stay there."

"Do you know, Hong Won, that nobody has ever been told that they were no longer needed in our village?" Young Kim's mother says. "No, we want Young Kim and Ki Jun to stay. We want them to stay and work, to play good music and to encourage our workers. We want them to do God's will. They play so well, and everybody in the village loves them, too! So, we hope they will stay with us for a long time. We always hope that—for them and everybody. Do you understand that, boys?"

"Yes," the boys answer, together. "If we could become Common-labor Farmers band members like Young Kim and Ki Jun, would we then always be playing and encouraging the people, too, just like them?" the older brother asks, speaking for both boys. "And would everyone in the village love us too, just like they love Young Kim

---

1. See next page.
changgo, a traditional, indigenous Korean hourglass shaped drum, typically used in folk music

and Ki Jun?" The quizzical boys are curiously expectant about her answer.

"You are a very smart boy, Hong Won," Young Kim's mother says, as she bends down and pats him on the back to give him encouragement. "Yes, if you do what they do, you will always play music, dance and sing, and everyone *could* love you. I do think they will. But, the love that everyone gives them is not only because they play in the Farmers band. No. It is the love that is in our village from *Hananim*, whose love runs in and through His people. And, it must be freely given to all, and be given correctly."

Spontaneously, the boys begin to march together, dramatically exaggerating every motion. Each boy takes the role of his older, band- member counterpart and role model. The boys smile with contentment about their new role identity as they gleefully march around Young Kim's mother, make instrument sounds with their mouths and vigorously play 'air drums'.

The elders from Kyung Jae's village have gone to meet with the leaders of the neighboring village in the home of one of the leading elders. They have already left when the group with Young Kim's mother, Miss Oh, and Ki Jun arrive at the school. The elders became engaged in preliminary discussions about the actual number of farmers who would commit to working to establish a new base for the collective labor force. The elders are interested in knowing details of how the society may differ from the generic capitalist or communist socio-economic lifestyles. These elders are basically traditionalist Koreans and they sincerely want to avoid the potential of political extremes.

At this time, they are not too interested about making decisions for radical lifestyle changes. These elders are more concerned with the welfare of the young ones of their village; those at risk. To have good teachers for their children is a very important interest for the elders, now. They all agree that it is an immediate and urgent need. Therefore, these discussions are important to the elders who want to know what workload will be necessary. The elders with Kyung Jae need to learn what percentage of the village's workers will join the work-fellowship that the two villages plan to form. Then, they will be able to figure the work-logistics for each village, and the villages as a unified whole. Only then will all the elders be able to decide unanimously to form a coalition, according to Korean tradition, and specifically for the collective work villages in Korea. That is imperative, in this case, too, to both parties.

As the group of teachers walk from their meeting at the school, they pass through the center of the village, through the street market and by the main commercial district. Ki Jun sees so many things there that are similar to what he sees so often in his village. He notices the same basic location of the commercial and market areas. He also notices that the size of the residential housing area around the commercial district is also about the same. Next, he notices one striking difference. This difference puzzles Ki Jun. That difference is the presence of the numerous solid-color green, red, yellow and blue flags scattered around, waving in the air. The flags fly on housetops from short poles.

Ki Jun is very curious about the flags, which elicits a nagging yearning to know within him. Since they are unfamiliar to him, he asks Chun Ja about it. She tells him briefly that they show the people that it is the residence of a village animist/folk religionist.[2]

He is clueless about why, but Ki Jun feels strongly impressed to ask again, this time *more* about the flags, which are new to his eyes. "I do not notice anything that really seems unusual to me, Ki Jun. The flags are in many neighborhoods in the city," she replies. "But, while in your village I sensed that something was not present. Yet, at the same time, I felt that something was 'more right'," she says, as she emphasizes the last two words. "Still, it did not take but a short while to realize the source of that mystery.

"At the sight of the absence of the flags, I began to ask myself about the amount of problems in your village," Chun Ja transfers her thought in a more positive direction. "I wondered if your village's way could be effective in overcoming problems. I did think that it might be. After that thought, I began to think deeply. Then, I thought of the afflictions of the nation—afflictions which affect virtually the whole land."

"What? What kind of 'national' afflictions?" Ki Jun asks, a little defensively. "Oh. Afflictions like divisions within the country," Chun Ja explains. "For example, not only the great dividing-in-half of the country by the tragic and bloody, war, wherein people kill distant relatives, but even in ancient history, in the Samguk era. You know—the *Three* Kingdoms of Silla, Paekche and Koguryo. There were fortified walls of division between the three kingdoms in what had been a once-unified land.

"So, our nation has suffered the inheritance of national-division, which can only be broken by moving

---

2. *mudang.*

with determination in the direction of unity and integrated acceptance of the other party, or parties," Chun
Ja explains.

"Even in villages of collective/fellowship farming,
division is seen. People who were slaves, or like slaves
in the poorer classes serve their owners or masters who
are also distant relatives," Chun Ja says. "That is a
secret of history which nobody speaks about, for it is
truly shameful. The shattered way has followed through
the years, even until today, in some places!" Chun Ja
emotes. "It is my sincere hope and belief that it will soon
be stopped."

Though uneasy, Chun Ja still enjoys talking with
Ki Jun as they walk. To talk in this way helps her learn
more about Young Kim, through Ki Jun. Chun Ja had not
planned to be explicit about her motives for talking to
him. She wanted to be friendly with Ki Jun, hoping that
he would thus be open to questions that she might wish
to ask him about his friend, Young Kim.

Ki Jun is not sure why Chun Ja is here, but he is
curious to know the reason. His mind is also influenced
positively by the communications with Miss Oh, in
which he was humbled. Ki Jun's earlier encounter with
Miss Oh is now reflected back in his mind.

At that same moment, Chun Ja plans a strategy. She
knows that there is but a short distance to the meeting
place, and she is careful to ask one important question
of Ki Jun.

She speaks warmly, but seriously, "Ki Jun, can you
tell me about how your friendship with Young Kim has
developed during the years? I mean, especially con-

cerning your involvement in the Co-operative-fellowship farmers band?" [3]

A week earlier, Ki Jun could have answered that question more easily. To take account of the events of the preceding week now leaves Ki Jun speechless, without the right words to answer simply, accurately and conclusively. He doesn't clearly know in his mind exactly what he has experienced. He sees the events as an extended time of calm and peace followed by a life-twisting cyclone or hurricane.

Finally, Ki Jun deduces his response, "Mostly good," he says. "Our friendship has been good, beyond all expectation, Chun Ja." Now Ki Jun is able to see for himself that his life was like a tiny model of, and personal re-enactment of the fractured state of his beloved homeland.

Ki Jun hesitates, while he thinks, 'That *is* a difficult question. How can I answer it?' Chun Ja interrupts before he can answer, "'*Good beyond all expectation*' is a strong and positive expression of a relationship which very few people can claim. Can something so strong be only 'mostly good'?" Chun Ja challenges the young man, while also hoping to encourage him.

Ki Jun hesitates again, and stammers, "Uh, well . . . ," even now, Ki Jun has no words to speak. He knows that many things found a new context in the past week. Such a context causes his mind to be stretched beyond its previous boundaries. It was being over-exerted, much like how an over-inflated hot water bottle would be stretched close to the point of explosion. Actually, he thinks, '*Over-exerted*'! This is more like how the thought- pic-

---

3. *Ture/Doorae nongak*

ture appears in his mind, which causes him to wonder, 'Is there now a new dynamic at work in this relationship?'

'No!' He answers himself, and thinks, 'There is now a new dynamic in life, and a new realization of the spiritual accountability of a person to right living and to his or her neighbor. This is what the results will be.'

No, although Ki Jun does not have words for the 'particular definition' of this relationship, he says, "I have now learned what I thought I did not have to know." And then, Ki Jun's words finally escape from his mouth. "I have learned a basic thing—a basic principle. I am learning who I was trying to be and who I was not, to better understand who I really am," Ki Jun reflects, orally, with a clearer mind. "Knowledge is necessary before I can know what I must do to respond correctly to another committed member of our community.

"Perhaps I have found the words for you, Chun Ja," Ki Jun says. "It is an ideal. The commitment means that in Korea, there must be total individual, inter-dependence in my and every other community."

"But, that does not say anything about Young Kim, personally. Please forgive me for having spoken indirectly. I know him as a very good man and a hard worker. We are both young, and not greatly experienced in life," Ki Jun proclaims, slightly embarrassed. "But I know that his heart is stable, and that he will do anything to see that the tradition is passed on; the tradition of committed community life which was handed to him as an inheritance.

"Those values are the same to which his parents have been committed for many years, Chun Ja. To work together in the fields and in a band does not produce an absolute guarantee of intimacy or a confident understanding of someone — or of oneself, either. I hope you follow my meaning."

Ki Jun is distracted by two small boys happily shouting and running toward them. As they move closer, he recognizes them. It is Chong Won and Hong Won, the two boys 'temporarily orphaned' by the recent accident on the road. "Hello, hello, Ki Jun!" the two shout enthusiastically. Ki Jun opens his arms toward the first boy as he runs into them and Ki Jun raises him up, high above his own head at arms length. "We were in a new music class today, at school," Chong Won laughs. "And our teachers are from your village — they are Common-labor teachers!"

The boys still have the thought fixed in their minds of becoming just like Ki Jun. They communicate this to him, with all confident expectation and excitement. Both of the little boys begin to drill Ki Jun with questions about his lifestyle in the Common-labor and Farmers band community. They repeatedly ask him, "If we learn our music very soon and practice very much, can we become a Farmers Band music and dance leader just like you?" All that Ki Jun can answer is that they will be capable sooner, as they study and practice 'without ever giving up'. The boys are encouraged, and Ki Jun tells them that he has arranged to take them to his village to be there during the Fellowship/common-labor group meeting.

"Do you boys feel energetic — enough to walk all the way to my village with me?" Ki Jun asks, with a persuasive tone.

"Yes, yes!" the boys immediately shout together. "We are very energetic," this time Chong Won answers for them.

"Good! Shall we race past the outdoor marketplace? Go!" he shouts without hesitation. Ki Jun quickly takes a few steps, leaving before the boys realize the race has begun.

Soon, in their excitement, the boys race past Ki Jun, who purposefully slows to allow them an encouraging lead. Near the finish, he runs hard to be even with the boys, so as to intensify and dramatize the finish.

From there, they begin the long walk back to Suwon-san. At the time, the small group of women walks past three clustered farm houses. The women are headed toward the marketplace. Mrs. Choi explains to the group about the surroundings, as they walk. The immediate area is where the almost-orphaned boys are being raised. She leads the group along a row of trees and stops just short of the location of the meetinghouse for the Common-labor, two-village council, and tells more about the immediate area.

While the group pauses in the shade of the trees, Mrs. Choi explains that the row of trees had once extended farther, but several large trees had been cut and burned for heat, in several, consecutive severe winters. She reminds all, who already know, that coal is used throughout all Korea for heating, but there has been an occasional simultaneous extreme cold and shortage of coal.

She explains that wood must be used in seasons of severe cold for more than just the primary house heating, as ancient tradition prescribes. It is well known that the cooking fire, at the inside corner of the house's 'L' shape, is the heat-source for the *sub-floor channels*[4] which dif-

---

4. *ondol*—an ancient, Korean invention; the sub-floor heating prototype of modern, central-heating systems.

fuse heat throughout the house. During a few past years however, wood was burned as well as coal—less efficient, but houses needed more heat against the biting winters' chill.

The trees mark most, though not quite all, of the property line. Otherwise, as in the past, one could walk the full length along the line of trees to find the house where the chief elders meet.

Just as the boys and Ki Jun walk past the women stopped by the trees, he notes two birds fly into one of the trees. What catches his eye is that these birds are unlike any he has ever seen. Neither are they like any of those of his village. Taking special notice of these birds, he chuckles to himself—partly at his own naiveté, and partly that he is surprised to see almost *anything* in nature which he has not seen, before.

"The world is bigger than one village," he says, verbalizing his thought, as he begins to briskly walk to stay apace with the enthused and expectant, scampering boys. After they leave the market area, Ki Jun can just barely hear Mrs. Choi instructing the women about the hoped-for attendance at the meeting which is scheduled to begin soon.

She asks, "Shall we proceed?" as she sees people returning from the meeting's break time. Inside the place of meeting an elder-statesman from Suwon-san's neighbor village begins to speak to the assembly. He says, "Not everyone here agrees with the plan that we join and integrate with the Common-labor way of farming and living. I, too, am one who has not yet fully decided to favor that big change for our village. It is clear to me that we would be giving away our right to be independent

and self-governing, as we have been for so many generations, and for the entire memory of our elders.

"Although, I do know," continues the white-haired
gentleman, "that this Common-labor life is not the plan
for every person of our village, it should still be a benefit
for those children who have been left without the protection of father and mother." As he speaks those words, a
faint, cheer-like noise of affirmation arises from the hall,
making a harmonious sound. The noise is mixed with
a kind of grumbling sound, like the sound of a tractor
which chortles and coughs — resisting an immediate start.

Young Kim's father then arises to speak, and the
room becomes still. "Because the people in the community are valuable to us in volunteer-labor life, we are able
to live more prosperously than from any other lifestyle
that is known to us." Kyung Jae speaks with compassion
and from deep within him. "Our economy is social. It
is spiritual. It has a value above money, above political
ideals, and above personal gain.

"As our Farmer band banner proclaims, 'Farming is
a gift of God'. *That* God is the God of Heaven. We will
always emphasize that our God is *Hananim*, the God of
our ancient ancestors. All must know, here and now, in
advance, that the Common-labor life is based on that
truth, and upon the reality that all property in the village
in reality belongs to this One; our God!

The room remains still. "The God of Heaven has
given us relationship with Him that is the model for our
relationship with one another. We keep good practices in
our personal lives and we clearly follow the right ways
within our community relationships, generally according
to our ancestors' traditions. In this lifestyle, there is
always somebody there to care for another who is in

need. I ask that you all please listen to one of the teachers from our village, who will speak." Now he introduces Miss Oh.

"Thank you, organizing leader[5]," says Miss Oh. "Thank you for the introduction." After she bows to Young Kim's father and the assembled group, Miss Oh says, "I am honored to speak to you here in this village; the neighbor of Suwon-san.

She begins and says, "First, I want to express our deepest sympathy to the entire village for the tragic injury of the fathers of the young children, here. Our hope is that you all will be given help, and given comfort in your hearts. We hope that we can do everything to help, which would not otherwise be possible for one village, alone.

"I thank you all for allowing me, not only as a woman, but young and unmarried, to stand before you and speak. My life is better each time that I can help others. Even in a sad and tragic time as this.

"There are teachers from our village who know that this is an opportunity to help with your urgent need here in your village," Miss Oh says. "We want to do it very much. We do not want anything in return, except we do hope that people here will be able to observe and see that this village can grow stronger. And, you will become more secure. It is our hope that when you let us come in and be like your employees, and your family, then you will understand, better. Yes, we will be like willing servants to you.

The room seems to shake as thunderous applause and a roar suddenly arise, in response to Miss Oh's words. It is totally unexpected and surprises most people, especially

---

5. *Yongjwa.*

the Suwon-san residents. They are surprised to realize that *they* are the enthusiastic ones. When the noise subsides, Miss Oh says, "We are thankful that we have the opportunity to serve your village. But, I want to say to everyone from Suwon-san, this is just the beginning. We will not stop with serving only one village. Please consider the word of God when He commands us to go into al the world, to take the Good News to every nation." Miss Oh expresses her thanks again, bows and returns to her seat near the front. The room buzzes with talk about how Miss Oh unexpectedly revealed this *Rhema* word from God.

The leading elders intently fix their gaze upon one another. The conversations die down and silence falls over the room like an ominous cloud. Now, the elders fix their gaze upon the eldest, who is the elder with greatest authority and influence in the village. As spokesperson, he nods his acknowledgement, stands to his feet, smiles, bows and begins to speak. "There is no need for further talk or discussion, in my opinion. I can see that we will accept your help, here. And I know you will succeed!"

Then, still smiling, he continues, "With one condition!" he exclaims. "We have discussed about what we have seen and done with you over the years. We do not have any great things which we hold against you. Still, to invite a new order and influence into our village in such an abrupt manner could be like leaving the door open with the ox standing nearby, in the field. It may decide to wander inside, here. So, the condition which we have decided to ask of you is to make an agreement to 'a time of testing' to work together. Then," the elder continues, "we will see and know how well your work and labor-fellowship life will benefit this village. It is not easy to simply open our door, as if blind, to a well-intentioned neighbor, in consideration of the great need we have in our village. But, you are welcome as long as no unethical thing takes place," the elder says. "If you agree, then come and begin the Volunteer-labor work, just as is done throughout the land. Come! You are welcome here!"

CHAPTER XIV

LABOR IS EXTENDED, HOPE FOR SOLIDARITY

Kyung Jae communicates to everybody in the meeting, about the warm invitation to the village given by the elder of the adopted neighborhood village. He says that there will be a demonstration of the Farmers music band of the Cooperative-labor Association. It will be a traditional celebration, in honor of the collaboration of labor of the two villages.

"This is not socialist labor or philosophy, but a free-enterprise system," Kyung Jae insists. "Unlike typical capitalism, however, the pursuit of money is not the highest priority. In the Fellowship-labor Association, *relationship* motivated by true and selfless love, with a work ethic, takes the highest place in the socio-economic system." Kyung Jae makes the point very clear, in case anybody in Suwon-san might think that there is going to be a change in policy for the integration of these two neighboring villages.

Next, Kyung Jae, without any anticipated, related hindrances, announces the music demonstration that has been planned. Moreover, he becomes aware—with Suwon-san—that a huge breakthrough in the spiritual realm has happened. The band's potential has just been increased immeasurably—as the conduit of the gospel in Korea, and to the ends of the earth!

As soon as he hears the announcement, a messenger quietly leaves through a side door to notify the band members to prepare. Meanwhile, the people in the meeting room begin to relax by introducing themselves to members of the other village. The new trans-village bonding of lives has begun!

At the same time, Ki Jun with the two boys is just turning from the main road to enter to where his house is located. They cannot see any houses yet, as the view is obscured by the thick growth of trees where the unpaved road turns in from the main road, which passes the edge of the village. The thick trees block them from seeing Cho Young, also. He is within hearing distance of Ki Jun and the boys, who walked the road from the next village back to Suwon-san. Suddenly, Cho Young appears before them. They are a little startled, but they quickly exchange bows.

Cho Young says, "I am sorry that I cannot stop to talk, but I have to keep an appointment to talk to Young Kim. He knows something very exciting, and I will tell you as soon as I see you—if the answer is positive."

Without hesitation, Ki Jun speaks, unable to conceal his excitement. "Let me quickly say to you, Cho Young, that I am taking these boys to see our village and to help them learn something of our life. Like you, they also have lived differently than we live, here. Have you seen anything interesting about this village?"

"Thank you for asking me!" Cho Young answers. "Yes, I can say that your lives may appear to be just as anywhere in Korea, but there are great treasures hidden in this village that others have not seen!" Cho Young speaks enthusiastically. "I will not say more, right now. I hope that I will see you soon. I have to go!" Then, he bows, and quickly turns and hastily walks to see Young Kim.

Ki Jun smiles and the three return the bow. They sense Cho Young's excitement, and the boys stare after him as he hurries down the road. They also smile, now sensing an unknown, common bond between themselves and Cho Young. They wonder, not knowing that their lives have already been placed into some of the most capable and loving hands in all Korea.

Ki Jun and the boys make their way to his house, each one excited about the shared adventure. As they arrive at Ki Jun's house, Cho Young continues to walk and draws closer to his destination. He considers carefully just what he will say to Young Kim about the radical choice he has decided to make, which will doubtlessly turn his life around. He does not know that the freedom with which he makes *this* choice was not available to the very man to whom he is to first reveal his thoughts.

As he approaches the house, Cho Young looks at the group of men coming out of it. They are coming out in groups of two and three, walking much slower than the normal pace. As Cho Young watches, each group seems to be locked in deep discussion.

Then, he sees Young Kim emerge with an older man, whom he guesses is a local villager. The next moment, Cho Young sees the man bow, turn and walk away. He sees his opportunity and Cho Young takes long, quick strides to Young Kim. He bows as he draws near. Young Kim returns the greeting.

Surprised, happy, and excited to see Cho Young, Young Kim allows him to speak. "I have done something radical, Young Kim," he breathes deeply, almost hypnotized by the excitement of the moment. "I have turned my back on that which, up to now, I have always loved!'

Now, the ones who have respected me for so long will not accept me once again as a friend. To them, I may now be their enemy, like a traitor to everything they love and respect."

Then, Young Kim listens and watches, seeing the mesmerized excitement in Cho Young's facial expression, yet not without a visible sign of remorse or pain.

He thinks he will help Cho Young with a question to make his abstract words more tangible and understandable. He says, "I think that it is clear to see that what you have always loved is farmers music and dance.[1] Isn't that true?"

---

1. *nongak*

"Yes!" Cho Young answers, confidently. "I have asked the band to give me time—at least a couple of days—to see if there is not a different, more fulfilling way; a better way to live."

"And you have come here for that!" Young Kim exclaims. "What is your plan, Cho Young?" he asks him. And he guesses Cho Young's answer in his own mind.

Cho Young glances around with some anticipation at the groups of men standing close by, most within a few steps of him and Young Kim. He feels both like shouting out, and coughing out a soft, embarrassed, whisper.

He does neither. Instead, he calms himself, and with all self control, he speaks. "I do not have a plan other than to tell you that I do not intend to return to perform with my farmers music band."

"It is a great sacrifice to leave such a life of secure things. I have to leave all of the excitement, the popularity, a deep well of talent, the opportunity to constantly explore new horizons in life . . ." and he stops with the sudden realization of his past actions and immediately begins to consider his words, deeply. He stands face-to-face with reality; "*A more real* reality," he blurts out. It is the reality of those things that *he thought he loved*—to leave them behind, for the very reason that he has tasted new, different and more meaningful things.

"These things are of *so much more value*—how awesome"—he realizes and verbalizes. Yet, he sees irony, for he also realizes that he was talking as if those recently forsaken ways are still more important.

Young Kim perceives exactly what Cho Young is thinking. He cannot imagine why he would think otherwise. "But, Cho Young, do you know that *our* values of this *Volunteer-labor community* [2] do not allow *us* to independently make the decision to quit our group; either the volunteer-labor association, or the association's Farmers music team?

"As so many decisions in this land are made in this manner, so we must consult those close to us." Young Kim continues, "We must consult our family members and village leaders. By mutual, willful, covenant agreements, we are not able to do what you have just done."

Young Kim is reluctant, for he is not yet ready to reveal that he and Ki Jun actually tried to do, in their village, just what he was telling Cho Young that they could not do! He too, 'realizes the shadows which follow him'.

"Individual decision making is something I considered a freedom, a benefit of the farmers music band life, Young Kim," Cho Young says. "Now I can see what *I thought* was freedom, is a lot of the breaking of an established and respected order; the order of centuries of valued tradition.

Our lives can become surrounded by such strong influences that we can no longer see clearly what is all around us," Cho Young shares the reactions of his thinking with Young Kim. "We lose focus and our sight. We become hazy-sighted, and then blind. Freedom becomes just another tool, and it is manipulated for use for our personal satisfaction.

"I could not see," Cho Young confesses, "that I had rejected the cultural traditions of my forefathers. I unknowingly began to reject and waste the good values that had been developed and passed along by good people, for so many centuries."

---

2. *Ture/Doorae*

"Such social blindness can darken the sight of more people in each new generation. And, it has struck this generation very hard," Young Kim agrees. "That blindness has even touched members of our own community," Young Kim admits, alluding to himself only vaguely — so as not to reveal his error, sorrow or shame.

Boldly, Cho Young asks, "Young Kim, do you have a place for me in the Common-labor community, and in your community's Farmers music and dance band?" He is vulnerable, but hopeful. "I have told my friends goodbye. If you have a place for me in this community, I will not need to return to the tour of the specialized farmers' music and dance band. No, I will not ever return." The hearts of both men are touched by the intense emotional impact.

"There *is* a need for more workers, Cho Young, as we have decided in the meeting that we will help the village next to Suwon-san with a portion of their farming," Young Kim answers, surprising himself at his openness. We also have a new direction of opportunity. Your timing is amazing Cho Young, because I just recently learned that *we* have not been living with the integrity as a Common labor Farmers band like we all thought we were. Now, we are being directed to travel to other villages — like the groups of Namsadang p'ae with which you have spent the greater part of your life!

"More immediately, our choices are motivated very much by the needs of the orphans, here. Yes, I believe we definitely can make a place for you; it must be decided by the village as a community. And, you must also learn and understand the structure of our Volunteer-labor community, and how it operates. Then, you must agree to commit to the ways of our community. Then, will you be totally accepted as a member."

Young Kim says, "Cho Young, this community lives according to the foundational principles of our ancestors. The individual is valuable, and he or she finds a more effective role as an active contributor to the whole community."

Young Kim continues, "The well-being of the whole community is most important; and now I realize that certain values of your life-until-now have been illuminated for us to see. So, the individual's worth corresponds not only directly to the group and not to their personal position, possessions, or popularity—but also in their sensitivity to listen, be teachable and obey.

"Like our ancestors, we also can find part of the source of our success in a social order. The order is that nobody is independent of, or in outright defiance of the community principles. That is so, even though we do not insist that anyone immediately commit to follow the God of our ancestors," Young Kim says. "But, ironically, the new call to travel outside of Suwon-san demands a heart after God[3]."

Young Kim adds, "After living among us, you will be able to see for yourself that life here is good, and it is unique. Then, you will be able to choose from what the voice of truth and reality speaks to you." With that, Young Kim feels peace with his words to Cho Young, and thus his overall relationship with him.

"Thank you, Young Kim," Cho Young says, overcome by emotion. "It is not an easy choice to make, to leave my friends and fellow performers—it is especially

---

3. *Hananim*

so; after working with them in so many places and for such a long time!"

"Do any of your friends expect you to return here, Cho Young?" he asks, carefully.

"Nobody said anything to me about this!" Cho Young reflects, still emotional. "And I was personally unable to say anything. Why? Because I would not have my friends know that I was turning my back on them. That is, Young Kim, even though anyone in farmers music and dance knows that a man can leave any group without shame. In specialized farmers music troupes, contrastingly, there is not the moral accountability as you practice, here. Thus, for me to leave is a matter of conscience. It is not of the conscience of a majority agreement, as in your common-labor association living—as you live here.

"Still, for me, leaving is not an easy thing to do!" Cho Young confesses.

"But, Cho Young, how can you leave your friends uninformed about a thing as important as changing your life and values? It is radical when you will be doing the same kind of thing, musically. How amazing it is that now, you may be living a similar lifestyle as before, but, with values and relationships most likely totally changed.

"Your friends must know that it is no small matter for someone to give up a lifestyle with many personal benefits to live a more orderly life!" Young Kim reminds Cho Young.

"I will tell you very soon, what I am going to do," confesses Cho Young. "I really was so sad to have to leave my friends. And now I will be content to be accepted into the community, Young Kim."

"You can tell of your desire, and then it is required that you proclaim verbally to the elders, and to the community, Young Kim instructs. "But, I welcome you now as a brother into the family. Come, let us go together and eat."

"Young Kim, *'yoboseyo'*[4]," his father called from a short distance, near the door of the meeting building, where he had been talking with a village elder. He slowly approaches to a distance of a few steps, and considers the time and the opportunity. "Please, do you have a minute, that we may talk?"

"Of course, father." Young Kim answers politely. "We were just talking about Cho Young's hope to become part of our community and about the necessary steps to secure it."

"You have a desire to become a community man—a volunteer-labor association, Farmers music and dance band member, now. Is that right, Cho Young?"

"Yes sir!" Cho Young enthusiastically answers, shouting with an almost military sound.

"We will be happy for you to work and live with us in our community." The Common-labor veteran encourages the experienced musician. "Did Young Kim tell you that this is not a simple, or light, commitment, but that it requires dedication and selfless sacrifice? That is not to say that this is a hard-labor institution. It is a place of fulfilling relationships and purposes, when we live up to our common ideals and our personal consciences.

"Of course, as a community, we are made to be a strong unit in faith.' Kyung Jae begins to expound. "That

---

4. 'Hello', a short greeting, typically used to answer the telephone—unlike the more formal and traditional greeting that communicates well being to you, *'annyong haseyo'*.

is, faith in the God of our early ancestors, who is the God of Heaven."

"Yes sir," Cho Young answers, again with a military-sounding response; with submission. "That is what Young Kim has just taught me. I am ready, sir!" Then, all three men laugh together.

"He has left behind the Specialized Farmers Music and Dance, with its influences of pagan religion, father. He has told me that," confirms Young Kim. With those words, Cho Young swiftly kicks at the ground, stirring up a small cloud of dust, to emphasize his zeal.

"Sir," Cho Young soberly says to Kyung Jae, to show respect, "I have lived a life full of excitement and adventure for some years. During that time I thought that I was working toward the establishment of a form of the performing arts, which has brought freedom to many in this country. Now, I know from my experience in the past days that I have seen only a small part of what is to be seen.

"Now sir," Cho Young continues, soberly, "I must see the sun rise, *and* the setting of the sun. To see only one without the other will leave a person without a clear vision of the daytime—and without a perspective. You are both so true when you say that Ture nong-ak, collective-fellowship farmers music, is not like that of a troupe of strolling actors. You have told me that Volunteer-labor Association Farmers Music and Dance is *not* like the combination of the noble 'hwarang' knights and warriors, and the ignoble, quasi-shamanistic and *male entertainers*[5]— with their amoral worldview!"

---

5. *kwangdae*

Cho Young kicks up another small cloud of dust, in secure confidence, and continues, "I believe that I had a part in contributing to the recovery of the male entertainers, from the unjust place on the list of the 'Eight Outcasts', which our country had labeled among the least worthy. But, that which I thought I was helping to recover was really not male entertainment; it was an imposing force directed by obsessive good intentions. It is what I would call 'social inertia. . .'

"Young Kim's father and Young Kim—I have been taking a ride on an outstanding train. It is a classic train—and I didn't know who the engineer was! It is a train whose destiny may be tragic. I could not see that, before. I must thank both of you and others in this community for helping me to see that. And, I must thank you for helping me to make a safe landing 'after the jump' from that 'express toward oblivion'. Thank you *so much.*"

"Cho Young," Kyung Jae says, "You will see more. It is more than jumping from a train with no destination. But, it is a matter of not only having jumped, but of then catching the train which runs the opposite direction, Cho Young," Kyung Jae instructs the man. "You just get up, run alongside and climb aboard that train, which is the *right train going in the right direction.*

The farmer sagely adds, "Do you know that we all became orphans, long ago, when the decree was issued, by which the sovereign King of China removed the opportunity, the action, and the right to pray; were not all China and Korea made spiritual orphans?" the father laments the critical, historical event. "Clearly, yes! Likewise, as the King appointed himself the sole person authorized and worthy of the privilege to pray to the God of heaven, he then removed inspiration in one's neighbor, which was a common legacy in these lands.

"Likewise, the role model of the father, from that of the Absolute, the Great One was lost as the family leader and spiritual guide," Kyung Jae, the gentleman farmer, continues.

"As volunteer-labor associations were abandoned by musicians, there remained a power structure of the professional performer as a new answer to the missing relationship. Do you understand that parallel? Is that too abstract? I hope that you will soon understand."

"Yes, I am gaining a new, clearer perspective, Kyung Jae," Cho Young says. "If one is riding on the train that is traveling in the right direction, may anyone on that train adopt an orphan? For, that is the train onto which I am ready to climb aboard, my friends."

Both Kyung Jae and his son stand motionless and silent to let these words sink into their hearts. Their eyes are fixed and their minds are jogged. They realize that what they are hearing is pure, simple Common-labor vernacular. The common-labor community has acquired another phrase. A phrase has been donated by a 'non-member', and many have benefited from it.

Young Kim and his father look at Cho Young. Amazingly, their eyes have some difficulty as they try to focus on the man! Why? The 'fog' of extreme wonder and appreciation had very likely glazed their eyes.

The next morning, Kyung Jae summons the family leaders and elders to come within the walls around his house and yard. He stands on the edge of a raised step beside the outer wall of his house, where all can see and hear him. He is ready to make the special announcement. Some move from behind the few fruit trees to take a better position.

Kyung Jae begins to speak. He says that the extended Volunteer-labor team for the next village is about to do something unusual. The team is to do an end-of-the-labor-season celebration there! The people mumble in amazement and surprise. Soon, they begin to buzz like a swarm of bees. Inspired by the news, they break simultaneously into joyful shouting!

"Yes, some of you have known since yesterday that we already made this decision," Kyung Jae addresses the people. "Others of you are only now hearing this."

"What does this mean?" he asks. "Yes, you are right. This means that our village will have our biggest annual festival! But, it will not be in our village. No! It will take place in another village, not in Suwon-san! We have been offered the site of the farm of the recently-injured father.

Kyung Jae realizes that he is as excited as the people. There is excitement in the air. He says, "We are going to have a 'resurrection' service, for all the orphaned children. The little boys will be given new life, which could have been lost forever. Each child will inherit more than one father. Each will be endowed with the committed, limitless love of the Great Father! That is so much more."

"They have a new family that is committed to them," Kyung Jae says. This is the civic issue that is closest to his heart. "But now, we will come forth to restore to these boys the value of the family. We will restore to these boys, to their village, and to Suwon-san!"

"Yes! To their own village!" he enthusiastically shouts. "And who has ever done this before? Maybe nobody has ever done this. Nobody! That day is nearing quickly, so we must prepare quickly!

"We will give our new friends a demonstration of hospitality and of Co-operative-labor life. They will see the last day of the work year. They will see this on the very first day that we come to their village to work as a *'Ture*[6] group."

"Let us give to them more than we have ever given to ourselves," Kyung Jae is speaking from deep within the heart of the community association to his neighbors' hearts. "We must earn the trust and respect of every man and woman of that village. We must win the favor and earn the love of those little ones who look to us for help. They are the ones who no longer have their parents. We go to celebrate with them—and for them."

Kyung Jae continues to talk to the gathered neighbors. "Our commitment is not to the plants we have planted, but it is to that which is produced by those plants," Kyung Jae again refers to the neighboring village. "Our commitment is a by-product of our choice to live under the rule of God, Hananim!"

"Watch what Our God will do!" Kyung Jae cries. The people cheer, and jump up and down, merrily dancing and turning in each others' arms. They know much work is ahead of them. Also, they hope that much joy and fulfillment will result! Everybody is excited about the prospects of the new addition to the community-family.

The work will be in a new location; and the school will have new children, unfamiliar to us and with deep needs. Like a strawberry plant or a grapevine with running vines, the community will now stretch forth its

6. Traditional, Korean Co-operative Labor Association(s).

fruit-bearing life to those around it! Excitement will come from the involvement of almost everybody from the volunteer-labor group.

Even Cho Young has a special reason for his enthusiasm. He is now willing to help one of the new, 'interim orphan' boys as his financial supporter. He wants to adopt the boy as a father who supports his child for the material needs of his life. Yes, Cho Young is also excited!

CHAPTER XV

TO WALK THE COMMON-LABOR PATH

"Yes, Ki Jun, I like animals so much," Chong Won answers the question posed to evaluate the boy's interests and capabilities. "And I have tended cows and oxen, a little."

"That is very good, Chong Won," Ki Jun says, an offering of encouragement. "And how about you, Hong Won. Have you had a similar experience as Chong Won. "Yes, we have learned many things together. We have also spent much time doing many things together, Ki Jun." Hong Won accepts the encouragement also offered to his counterpart.

"Good!" Ki Jun passes his enthusiasm to the boy. "Then you can begin now. You are now officially our new *'pangmokkam'* our new 'herdsman, in training'. Come, and I will show you which way the oxen must go to walk to the field to eat. And, I will show you where they go to plow the field," he says. He leads the boys as they walk along the winding bank of the rice paddy. "See the little ox?" he asks, pointing to the animals. "It is less than a year old, and the one next to it is her mother. The other two brown ones are brothers of the little one's mother. We call the little one, 'Sijo'."

Ki Jun feels more relaxed to learn that the boys have some experience with animals. He steps aside to the small shed where tools are stored. He takes a wooden rod in his hands.

"This stick is only used to remind them to keep order and to not become unruly," he says as he turns toward the boys. "See the flexible tip? I just gently touch the ox on the side with this, and they will turn when they feel it. *Half of your job is* simply to watch the animals and to keep them from eating the produce of the field.

"Here, Chong Won. Please take this rod and walk alongside the oxen to guide them," Ki Jun says as he hands the rod to the boy. "We will continue along the bank until we pass that row of trees. That is where the oxen will stay to feed. Then, we will stop by the house, over there."

Everything proceeds without any hindrance, and the boys happily share the job of keeping the oxen on the path. After the oxen go to graze, Ki Jun calls to the house as they approach. He goes to the door, which opens as he nears it.

Two small drums, which belong to the band, are handed to him, with a little drumstick. *"Thank you"*[1] he says to the indistinguishable figure—unrecognizable to the boys through the cracks in the boards of the door.

"Which of you boys wants to play the drum with me?" Ki Jun asks, knowing that they both will eagerly volunteer. "I am holding a number of fingers out on my hand behind this little '*sogo*'[2] drum," he says as he extends two fingers, while holding the two small drums by their wooden handles.

"Two," Chong Won, shouts excitedly.

"Three," Hong Won echoes the next moment.

"Okay! Chong Won wins," Ki Jun shouts in response. Then, he dramatically pulls the hidden fingers into clear view for the boys to see.

Chong Won then shouts his joyful approval. He takes the drumstick and the small drum. Following the communities' '*we* principle', Ki Jun picks up two old metal plates beside the door and gives them to Hong Won, and says, "Here is your gong!"

"So, now we can all play our instruments!" They begin an impromptu session of "Let us sing a traditional

---

1. *Kamsa hapnida.*

2. Small, hand-held, stick-handled, Korean drum used in folk music.

song, boys. I will teach it. Listen closely as I sing one
time. Then, we will all sing together. It is easy. There are
only two lines. After I sing one line, we will sing it again
and again. Then, we all do the same with the next line.
Okay?"
He sings;

'It's raining; take the straw mat and put it over the
ox'.
"Okay, let's sing that line again and again. Sing with
me!"
'It's raining; take the straw mat and put it over the
ox.'

Now, the boys join the singing with loud voices.
"Good! You will become good animal keepers, *and* good
Ture, nongak players. Okay, the second line. Are you
ready?"

'It's sunny; take the straw mat off the ox.'

"Good. Okay now let's sing it several times." And Ki
Jun leads the boys in singing this verse.
When they had sung it several times—with jumping
and delighted dancing—the boys carefully keep an adequate rhythm on their instruments. Then, they stop, and
Ki Jun comes closer to the boys and says, "Chong Won
and Hong Won, both of you played, sang and danced like
truly good team members. I know that you will truly be
great contributors to the *Ture* community. Do you like
your first day of training for the common-labor life?"
Together the boys squeal a loud, "Yes." "Now you have

learned how to talk to one another about your work—to talk by using a song!

"Now you are both experienced workers. And, I think that you have done a great job!" Ki Jun says. "I thank both of you for your hard work and courageous efforts!" With that, Ki Jun gives them both a big, fatherly hug and takes the instruments back to the doorway, where the unseen person takes them from Ki Jun's hands. The two boys laugh as they watch when the figure disappears quickly into the shadow. They look at one another, smile, and turn happily to follow Ki Jun back toward the oxen and home. Both boys now belong to the family of laborers! And, the two boys feel a new, clean feeling by having taken part; even a small, beginning part, in the production of food for the Suwon-san *Ture* community.

CHAPTER XVI

LAST DAYS COME, FIRST DAYS GO

"Wow! Chong Won, not even a week has passed since we have been in this *Volunteer-labor group*"[1], Hong Won says as he stacks weeds in the field beside his bigger brother. "Already, I feel as if this is the life I was always meant to live—*forever*," Hong Won adds, wistfully emphasizing his final word.

---

1. *Ture/Doorae*

"I feel the same as you, Hong Won." His brother smiles as he replies and continues to work alongside him with his' youthful expertise', removing weeds from the field with a hoe.

"Boys!" It is Cho Young who laughs as he calls, for the boys to 'get to work'. By that, he means that he wants the boys to enjoy their time in the field, and to begin to learn to do the job with song and play, to encourage the other workers.

It is now late and the last official day of the work year. And then comes the biggest day of celebration. That special day is the day that everybody brings their hoes to wash, and stores them for the next year's work. It is a day of great celebration, about which the boys have repeatedly heard much talk. The boys are preparing themselves and are very excited about the day. They know, too, that there is a huge banquet for the entire village. Chong Won especially is very excited!

A single word from Cho Young is enough for the boys to stand erect and begin to walk toward him on the paddy's bank. Cho Young waits on the bank for them, with their drums at his side. The boys are very polite and obedient; moreover, because they see two other men standing beside Cho Young on the bank. They recognize Ki Jun, and beside him is Kyung Jae.

Everyone bows and exchanges friendly greetings to one another. Cho Young is ready to get started, and Kyung Jae wants to help him by making an announcement about the events of the next day.

But, the presence of the one who has crossed over from his longtime lifestyle to 'the other side' has left Kyung Jae momentarily without words. Kyung Jae has a profound sense of some uncertain thing being very good about what is happening here.

"Remember," he says confidently, and to encourage Cho Young, "this is *the day of washing the hoes*[2], and tonight is the full moon of the seventh month. This is the time when *everybody* sings and dances! It is a very, very big day." He shouts out his words and smiles broadly at the boys.

"Harvest time is near, boys," Cho Young says to them, hoping to stimulate them. "And next month the women will be preparing food that is sooooo delicious, including pears, chestnuts, persimmons, and pine nuts! And boys, there will be wrestling matches and sports." This last thought causes the boys to raise their eyebrows with interest. "And remember, everybody will wear clean clothes." Then, Cho Young bends down and speaks in a whisper to the boys, "Everybody does that; the farmers will work, and then they will come and play, dance, and sing. But, all will have clean clothes to add to the quality of the celebration."

"We need to practice," Cho Young encourages the boys. "For, it is an important day of celebration for the farmers. It is before the harvest, and the farmers will all be ready to celebrate the end of the work season. Then after one month, comes the festival to celebrate the providence of God. The farmers will celebrate joyfully with all their hearts!"

"Okay, remember the simple song that we learned together? This song is our song of encouragement! Let us start now and sing 'the ox song'," Cho Young says, and begins to lead them in singing.

---

2. *Homi ssishi*

Together they sing;
"Yippee! Yippee!
Here it is very good!'

Then, Cho Young lets the boys sing the verse alone, taking the opportunity to admire their happy anticipation. He reflects to himself that it is good that he taught them a short song. And this song has been sung from ancient times, used as a military marching song. But, Cho Young saw a new way to apply that kind of song. He transformed this traditional, processional song for a new song of marching; for a victorious march in the battle over the dark cloud of abandonment that can hover over so many people.

Again, the boys sing;
"I will follow him, I will follow him
Now that we've grown to love each other
I will certainly follow him.'

As they sing the boys are jubilant, and Cho Young joins in their joy and realizes how much more the boys will love it if they have an experience of this song—for the celebration. He thinks of the benefit because he knows that they will be joined by men standing in a line, with a line of women opposite them—all joining together to sing. All will have mulberry wreaths on their heads. The boys will also be crowned. There will be royal crowns of welcome, symbols of honor and welcome for the new members of the community.

Cho Young wants to shout as he thinks of an even greater thing. The boys will follow one of the oxen, which will be adorned with a colorful blanket, and Young Kim or Kyung Jae will ride it. Even now, excited anticipation fills the air, as well as every heart. For good reasons, the whole day of the washing of hoes is loved by all.

Not coincidentally, the celebration of 'washing of hoes day' is a special time for all. For the newly adopted boys it will be especially extraordinary. Why? Because they are not jut adopted into a family, but they are formally adopted as active, participating members of the whole community-family. It is a complete and whole relationship. And, according to tradition, they are to be literally called *'relatives'*[3] by everyone.

"Your adoption is a tradition which all Korea rejoices over! You are called *relatives* because you are brought in as a real part of the family," Ki Jun adds. The boys feel good because they know that they are fully *accepted* relatives and realize the comforting feel of the warm love.

It is not recorded that the *troupes of strolling actors*[4] *have* this tradition. No. The boys are happy and content to have been simply adopted into this growing, community family.

Chong Won and Hong Won are indeed happy, and somewhat overwhelmed as newly welcomed members of the community. And they are excited and filled with anticipation. However, the loving welcome totally precludes all their anxiety. The promises of the washing of hoes day fill their minds.

Amid the village's enjoyment of the delicious food, which Chong Won savors in no small quantities, the boys are presented with their wreaths. They are given their

---

3. *Tonggori*
4. *Namsadang p'ae*

crowns of welcome and honor before all the cheering people.

Wonderfully and incredibly, they are invited to begin at the top of the honor scale!

For, the tragedy of one village is the open door of opportunity for its neighboring village to use adoption of the other village in various ways.

Many consider this very unusual. People of any village can very often be suspicious of musicians of other villages. But, this triumph over adversity is proof positive. It is a demonstration that the *exception* of that suspicion is true.

Before the boys' ceremony of initiation as herdsmen begins, the 'Specialized Farmers Music Band' leader, Jae Kyung finds Young Kim to talk. He left the group's itinerary of travel for this information-gathering interview. He has come to see just what is—or seems to be—so different, and so good, that it could draw his companion to leave the group and turn away from a life of self-confessed, indulgent 'creative abandon'.

"Isn't your group performing somewhere, for the occasion of this ancient, traditional rural custom which remembers the lunar calendar *Mr. Band-leader*[5]?" Young Kim asks with innocent curiosity. "Your performances have deep roots in the cultural history of our nation," he politely offers.

"Thank you, but we have band members who have worked so hard," answers the band leader, with a slight tone of variance in his voice. "There is one or two who are not in real good health, just now. Therefore, it is a time of rest for us. Everyone needs a time of rest, correct?

5. *Sangsoe*

"But I am most interested in seeing my performing companion, Cho Young, again," he answers with sincere honesty. "As I said, I am so interested to see what he loves to do more than what we have loved to do, together, for so many years."

"Do you have an idea what could be the great attraction for Cho Young in this village, Mr. Band leader?" Young Kim asks, hoping to help Jae Kyung think in broader terms. Jae Kyung does not, but answers, "Has Cho Young now found the woman he will marry? I did not expect that. That is not something I would have readily expected of him!"

"No, this is about more than a woman," Young Kim says, engaging much self-control. But, every woman and man here has just what Cho Young came here to find; that is, the true value of life. Here, we are able to freely ask real-life questions.

"And, we are open to hear the answers, and to use those answers as actual guides to fulfilled living. Do you understand what I am saying, Mr. Band leader?" Young Kim asks sincerely and with rhetorical insight. "Here, there is love that does not stop when it 'full-fills' a person. The love does not stop—even when it fulfills others while it also fulfills the first person.

"How can we forget the group value which our ancestors have prized so highly for thousands of years?" Young Kim asks.

"There is love which comes down from above and is able to make every individual fully bonded to the group and to the whole community. It is a love that seeks to accomplish good for all—it is the love that has no limit;

it can only come down from the heart of *God the Father*[6], the Creator and God of everything. Only the love from such a great and big heart can satisfy us, and *only it and He* can fulfill us all."

Jae Kyung does not really hear all of what Young Kim says, which proves the rhetoric true by his answer that he does not know what question a person might ask, and why they would come here to ask a question.

"But I can see that your life has times of enjoyment. This village has made me very welcome in your community and I have been to some villages where our band and I were not welcomed. That is because I could not decipher some of the village's own Chinese-Korean lexigraphs. For that reason, visiting bands have been considered unworthy visitors. So, they are not welcome to enter that respective village," Jae Kyung says, without displaying any visible emotion.

"We do not celebrate every lunar month, Mr. Band leader," Young Kim says. "But here, we remember those and honor those who honor all, including the lowly. We will honor *them* more greatly than those who exalt the past more than the present life."

"Thank you for your opinion, our *lead singer*"[7] answers Jae Kyung, seeming uninterested. "You might ask me an important question when I come again. But, first I must take time to consider the important values of life, and what question, or questions, will come forth from them."

"Yes, excuse me Mr. Band leader, for I must go to ride the cow," Young Kim says with a smile, now cog-

---

6. *Hananim Aboji*
7. *Solsori*

nizant of the time. "I have been honored to ride as the *representative* of the field worker who *is actually being honored*. Like your group, he has worked so hard that he cannot attend the celebration, today. It is *he* who deserves the honor of riding the draped cow today, instead of me."

"I will consider the questions, Mr. Lead singer" Jae Kyung bids his counterpart, as he turns to leave. As he leaves, he speaks politely, yet with sounds like scorn blended into his voice.

Soon, Kyung Jae is in the midst of the festivities. "To our relatives, we give you the best we can," he announces to all who stand there watching. He now holds the cow by the rope tied loosely around its neck. The cow stands still for this honorable event, and only turns her head when the *large gong*[8] sounds. "The old proverb says that the secret to happiness is health, wealth and many sons," Kyung Jae announces. "Now, we are happy to welcome you into this community family, as *our* sons. And you are true contributors to the health of our community. Now there is nothing that will create distance between us.

"Chong Won and Hong Won, we welcome you today also as new members, and each of you as valued new herdsmen." Then, the people cheer loudly and begin to dance. Some leap into the air and shout for joy. The Farmers Band plays a song with a fast rhythm. Kyung Jae hands the rope to Chong Won, and the boys receive their crowns of welcome with joyful smiles.

As Kyung Jae begins to lead the boys down the road, Chong Won asks if they might first speak to Young Kim. Permission is given and Chong Won hands the rope to his brother as he begins to speak. "We are so thankful for

8. *ching.*

this day. We have learned so many good things only from seeing how you live your lives in this village. Already, you have given us so much. All we can do is to thank one of our leaders by giving him a small gift.

"This is for you, Young Kim," Chong Won says as he turns and looks atop the cow, where the substitute worker-of-honor sits under the warm summer sun, in the place of the too-exhausted-to-participate honored worker.

"Please listen," Young Kim responds. "You will see what we will be doing in the field." As the boys prepare to sing, everyone readies themselves to accompany the singers on their *Farmers music band* [9] instruments. The boys each pull out a piece of paper from under his waistband. They look at each other, then to the paper and back, once again. Then the boys begin to sing. They sing and read that which they have written by the special tutoring of Miss Oh. She has given them each a tool, and some loving attention.

As the boys sing, people begin to dance once again, accompanied by the team. However, these events come as a complete surprise to Young Kim. He knows that the whole village participates in the *washing of hoes day*. Then, he recalls that this is also the biggest festival day of the year. Still, he is surprised by the honor, and he is being honored, after all.

The two boys begin to lead the singing, shyly at first, and soon they joyfully sing;

'Come all men, our countrymen
0 farmers hear our words'

---

9. *Ture/Doorae nongak.*

The boys smile as they sing this work song of encouragement which they have learned. As the people dance, they all join the boys to sing the next chorus;

'At the sparrows' morning call, arise!
Shoulder your tools, lead out your ox,
Call your neighbors, your companions,
Come to good earth with the farmers' song
"Uh lull lull sangsa duiya'.

Now, the boys are touched in their hearts that they are able to learn a farmers' song from the ancient past and to be able to present it to the lead singer as a symbol of honor. According to tradition, it is the lead singer's responsibility to teach the two new herdsmen to sing songs for their job.

As they begin to learn, in the spirit of the Volunteer-labor Community, they are immersed in the midst of a community with a mature understanding of 'the spirit of adoption and love,' a gift from the D*ivine Father*[10], who gave the 'gift of agriculture' to the land of Morning Calm—and to the entire world. The farmers dance, the music continues, and becomes both louder and livelier. Everybody is very joyful about the adoption celebration, and they celebrate with nearly wild enthusiasm.

Cheers of *'well done'* and *'bravo* [11], and O.K.' are given the boys for their gracious and bold 'debut', and for their presentation of this new song. They sang as if they have been singing the song for years.

---

10. *Aboji Hananim*, literally, 'Father God'.
11. *Cho-ta!*

Everybody continues to dance and sing together, since the entire village has come to sing, to play instruments and to dance in celebration—on this *day of washing hoes*. The boys are excited and they talk among themselves and among the people.

Chong Won holds his small drum. It is now his prized trophy, and he says to his bother, "Hong Won, I am so happy—but we are so sad that our father is so badly hurt. It is better, because now he is being helped. Why? Because we have a new father—not just one father, but we have many men here who love us and are a father for us. I have a happy heart, and peace. And, Hong Won, the people talk about *another* Father, too—the Father of all, who loves all!"

All during this time, Chong Won and Hong Won are overjoyed at the opportunity to join with the *Volunteer-labor Farmers* Music Band [12] with no unexpected delay or problem. With his small drum in hand, Chong Won ecstatically accompanies the band! Hong Won is also ecstatic, and he, too plays along with the band.

Others, who dance and sing alongside the two young newcomers, smile warmly at them, with a welcoming spirit and love. They know that this is a very unique day, and that these activities must be unique, too. They also know that there are great differences in matters of faith and lifestyle in the farmers music world. Significantly, Common-labor Farmers music is distinguished from 'specialized Farmers music and dance' throughout history.

---

12. *Ture/Doorae nongak*.

One important reason is that there is an exclusive characteristic about the band about which the adopted boys know nothing. Since they are brand new members, they are naïve of that exclusive characteristic. A special name had been given to the band. The name *'pung jang'* was given to bands which are with the Volunteer-labor Farmers. As the boys play, they do not know or realize as they participate, that, in its original form, the Common-labor association–life is not complete without its Farmers music and dance. Though young and innocent, they dance and play together with many others who joyfully celebrate the day.

The boys actively enjoy their newly adopted family so much, and will learn in the following years about the things which will bring fulfillment and truth to their lives. They will be enriched with historical insights about the life they have and will come to live, enjoy, and love.

The community helps the boys understand about Farmers bands heritage. The term *'pung jang'* has been taken from an ancient composite term for 'the wind'. The boys are taught the important fact that this kind of band accompanied the volunteer-labor teams. They would travel around the countryside on the farms and play for the entertainment of the people. Without this musical accompaniment, it is said that there is no truly traditional Common-labor Association. The word literally means 'wind' or 'a big catch of fish'. This refers to ancient sea-fishing groups, and it is the basis for the logical, necessary union of the two entities.

This wind is a refreshing breeze that blows through the Volunteer-labor village. It is the Breath of life. It has been seen even to empower the open heart of *Common-labor* through that wind—a spiritual wind.

Those who are led to search and find the source of the Breath of life are ones who lead lives that are carried forth by the breeze of the limitless power of the Father's Spirit. That parallel 'father spirit' conceived and begat Tangun, a type whom the Kogum book calls 'Hwan-woong'.

This is the same breath that breathes life into Common-labor societies when the community is committed to following the higher ways of life. Those are the ways of God, The Great One, and the Son whom He sent to die in the place of all people.

This wind—this breath—was given a purpose from the start. The purpose is that which gives distinction to 'pung jang' from any other musical farmers' performance. This great wind exists in Common-labor Farmers music for the specific cause to encourage and raise the spirits of the living community. So has it been for centuries.

Everybody sees many villagers on this festival day that they would otherwise see only rarely. There is excitement among all the people, for that reason, besides many others.

Kyung Jae takes advantage of the opportunity to share with some hard-working farmers. He sits and tells them, "Sincere and genuine Farmers music and dance, of the kind that our village enjoys, must encourage the workers. This is the nature of our life. To share enthusiasm with others each day has priority, and has a purpose above personal gain. It is my hope that we have achieved our goal. For, by helping to remove stress from daily, hard work with this Farmers music band, is a wonderful and fulfilling part of our lives. The men surrounding Kyung

Jae all nod their positive response, trying to hide their appreciative smiles.

But, Kyung Jae knows that the band is not a group of 'professional encouragers'. No, but they are willing co-laborers who give others more than they would receive form them, if circumstances were reversed.

"Thus," Kyung Jae continues, "the highest common-good cannot be found without that kind of enthusiasm." The farmers and all the workers for the *'hoe washing day'* celebration are fully enthusiastic. The enthusiasm spreads throughout the village as the band plays traditional songs. They also play during the dramas, and for entertainment.

This is a time that the villagers eagerly anticipate, excitedly hoping with great hope. This day has special meaning to Kyung Jae. After the men move away to take part in a drama, he talks with Ki Jun, who then passes by Kyung Jae, ready to play the lead, *small gong*[13] .

"*Mr. Leader* [14]," Ki Jun says respectfully, "this day is a symbol of unity in the co-operative life that we live here." Kyung Jae nods, and asks affectionately, "Do you know what an important part of the unity is? It is that we all eat *the common meal* [15] *together*, not separately! It is followed by a time of rest. We share a meal—as a group and with a common heart! We do not even rest as individuals with personal agendas."

"Ki Jun," Kyung continues, "Ideally, everybody works for the good of one another, and so we have the opportunity to stop and eat together in the fields. We have

---

13. *kwaenggwaeri*

14. *Sangsoe.*

15. 'wet *chori'*

said why this is a special day, today. For us, today is the last day of the regular work season. But, more special, is that for Suwon-san's neighboring village, this is the day of new life. They, our neighbors, are held in respect by people all around. Otherwise, they may become vulnerable to a number of hindrances. We may also be vulnerable. We must not let that happen. But, we must always confess that it is only with the help of the Great One that we prosper."

"Now, my appetite tells me that there is no Common Labor association without common meals!" Kyung Jae laughs, with a broad, boyish smile.

Ki Jun is finished listening and he turns to join the Farmers band, which plays while the children dance. "These children would stand on the shoulders of the older men and would dance there, aloft, above solid ground," he says.

"Historically, these dancers were used as a cover for subtle espionage activities. They would form a pyramid on the shoulders of the men. It is this pyramid formation which brought the name of spies to the children, who were perched on many men's shoulders, long ago. The origin of the practice was traced to military times where sentries would take a high vantage point to watch enemy movement.

As the children dance, across the way, the freshly butchered and bar-b-que'd beef is being served to the people on the celebration grounds. Nobody is forgotten, including the widows, or the sick, even if they have not contributed to the labor.

One old man from the other village hobbles slowly up to the line where the food is being served and screams at the server, "What do you strangers think you are doing? Get out!" Abruptly, but slowly he then leans down and turns around on his bamboo cane. Next, he reaches for a bowl of rice, which he lifts to throw in the face of the server. Just beside the woman server, there is a flat, low and very wide tree stump. Only a short distance away from it is a large pot of rice. The server now ladles meals from the large pot into bowls as people pass by in front of her. She stops and quickly jumps on the stump, smiling a big smile, and she proclaims for all to hear, "This is a time, and an event, and a life that is," then she pauses and shouts, "justified! This life is redeemed; it is sanctified; paid for, and it is right! This life will be right, as we live it the right way! Thank you," she says, bows lowly and jumps down from the stump. She regains her balance and resumes in her role as the food server. Many people sitting at the tables nearby look up and nod their agreement. Others laugh.

As this happens, a small woman who is watching and hearing the woman on the stump speak, reaches forth her hand and restrains the old man who wants to accost the food server. "No, *daddy*[16]. Please! These people are our friends." The women who serve are delighted to serve the lesser able, even if problems arise. Thus, they help to bear some responsibility for the well-being of the entire community. They hope that there will be nobody forgotten, and that all might be served.

"They are also our neighbors," the woman says, as she releases the man. "And they are GOOD neighbors. Come, let us go and sit where we can eat together with

16. *Oppa*, Korean familiar term for Daddy.

the group." With that, the harmless old man smiles, follows his daughter and forgets his problem.

CHAPTER XVII

IS THIS THE BANNER OF AGRICULTURE —OR OF LOVE?

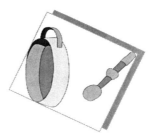

The banner of the Common-labor Farmers is important. It displays the sincerely held values of the community—the values that serve to uplift and hold the community together. The band brings forth the banner to the place where and all the people and the Farmers music band are gathered together in the cleared dancing area not far from the eating tables. The banner's pole is pushed deep into the ground where it will stand stable.

This banner is more than simply a traditional banner, for it reads; *'Righteous Farming Is the Basis of a Healthy World'*. The elders and the community have approved this banner. It proclaims the respect that the community has for the land and its provision, the subsequent health of the people of the community, and more so, for the Divine Giver of that great bounty.

Kyung Jae would see his son live to be very old and be still very strong, because this community—as well as much of the country and the world—is learning the secrets of *pre-modern* farming. In a time of self-reflection, he sees how so many aspects of the modern farming and ranching systems pollute the purity of the created order, and the food supply. Kyung Jae smiles and feels content as he watches the men and the children dance— and they all dance. The men and boys, the women and girls are essentially all so healthy. They eat mostly good, pure food, and live a good lifestyle of work and giving. They know that they are recipients of true, great riches.

Kyung Jae looks at the people, his heart is warmed and he smiles. As he watches them, they appear strong and healthy looking, now. Then, he marvels as he considers that while he acknowledges that even as they work so hard, they do not complain and they do not seem to become exhausted.

The farm leader thanks the Great One that he is a farmer and his village is in great health, enough to work hard, and to play unrestrained, with boundless enthusiasm!

As *the village organizer* [1], Kyung Jae prepares to announce the rest of the events of the day. The people

---

1. *Chipsa.*

are resting, and he announces that a traditional, *hunter's drama* [2] will be presented, and that all of the farm workers will take their hoes home this day, as this is the day designated as the last day of the working season. In the past, the women were not traditionally involved in this day of partnership. But now, in this *community of partnership*, they play an important role in the preparation of the celebration feast, and serving everybody. It is not repetitive to the people to be reminded that this is the biggest festival day, and that these women work so hard to please everybody!

The women are appreciated so much. That appreciation is manifested by Young Kim, who has written a special song—a *thank you* to all those who have worked to prepare and serve the meal. Moreover, the song is a thank you to all involved in the festival preparations and serving. Young Kim looks and sees that his mother serves the stew with Miss Oh. His mother says, "Is next month the month which we will celebrate *the women's dance* [3]?"

"Yes," Miss Oh answers with expectant anticipation. "And I am so happy to dance under the most beautiful full moon!" And she recalls how she and her mother-in-law first met.

"May I tell you how wonderful it is to live here as a part of this group?" asks Dan Bae, Young Kim's mother. Miss Oh nods her assent.

"We know there are things which help rescue this village from the ordinary life of seeking personal gain and believing that 'things' are so important. What rescues us

---

2. Pos'u.
3. *Kanggangsullae.*

is that we see mercy in our lives, and we see that it works to change our lives. When we are merciful to others, we also receive great mercy. Their conversation is edifying, and the women like to talk as they serve the hot *stew*"[4].

Dan Bae bows her head to each person she serves as she offers her service with a ladle of stew. Hers is a beautiful and humble heart, indeed. And, she silently prays for the weaker ones as they pass by.

"We are social equals here in the village. Not because some do not have better and varied abilities, Miss Oh," says Dan Bae. "The reason we are equal is that everybody has one *prioritized* purpose, here. That purpose is to see that everybody in the village succeeds in their work and in their lives. If everybody has not succeeded, then neither has the village fully succeeded."

Then, Miss Oh says, "Excuse me Young Kim's mother. May I ask you how can a — little dance, predominately for women, affect everybody's success?" Dan Bae responds with a question to elicit her future daughter-in-law's considered response. "What is your thought? What significant thing does the dance commemorate that is useful for the whole village?"

"A very good question, Miss Oh," the older woman says, as she moves closer in the food line. "It is just as in the days of Hideyoshi's naval invasion, when the women made a vital contribution to the defense of the nation when they danced. They moved about like busy supply troops, and danced around the large bonfire to deceive the attackers into believing that there was a great defense mounted against them! They took an equal responsibility

---

4. chigae.

as the men who did the actual fighting in the naval ships, there at sea."

"The women danced around a fire, and men were stationed aboard naval warships; this is an example of partnership and solidarity for the good of the land." "Yes, very clearly so," Miss Oh responds.

"Then, you see that women really do have a place that is important, and that they have saved valuable lives," Dan Bae says, more to the point. "They do their part to encourage the whole village, each day. They contribute all that they can. In times of greater need, they do just as the men do when they are called to a greater-than-usual need. "Yes, it is the patriotic spirit," concludes Dan Bae. "It is the same spirit that holds us from seeking personal gain and believing that 'things' are so important. What rescues us is that we see mercy in our lives, and we see that it works to change our lives. That is, when we are a country together in hope." As she speaks, the last few people pass their station and they ladle out the last portions of stew form the big, serving cauldron.

"That hope is so infectious," Miss Oh says. She receives the encouragement that she needs from the woman with more life experience than her. "This is a great day for my hope!" she cries, and jumps for joy.

"There will be an announcement today," says Dan Bae. "Yes," smiles Miss Oh. She could utter no more, as she is also surprised. She is overwhelmed with the hope of exciting fulfillment.

Chong Won and Hong Won sit together after they have enjoyed the delicious stew that the entire village has eaten and enjoyed, together. Just then, Miss Oh walks across the grounds toward the boys. The ground is carpeted with fragrant pine-needles and her steps are lightly padded. When she arrives next to them, she sits opposite them on another large flat-topped stone. This stone is shaped like a bench—the perfect shape for Miss Oh to sit upon. She is prepared to encourage the boys and to welcome them as new members of the fellowship community.

Miss Oh looks directly at the boys and asks them, "Do you boys know that the Farmers music and dance group of Common-labor, like ours, is very limited in this country?" Then, she moves on the rock to a place where she can sit closer to the boys, to be more easily heard. "Groups like this group are so limited that not too many people know that they have even existed.

"So many people have heard popular tapes of specialized farmers music. They also believe that the pervasive Buddhist and folk-religionist rites are exclusive characteristics of the farmers music style. But, boys, *we* are living proof that what so many people have heard is more myth than truth. It is not really true, at all."

As she has an important 'end point punctuation' to communicate, Miss Oh adds, "For that reason there has been great hindrances of the musical development of the Farmers music of the past. Past societies of shared-labor in our tradition were hindered. We are still able, but not of our own power, to overcome all hindrances against us." Miss Oh says this because she hopes to inspire the boys. "What can anybody do to help the growth of our Farmers music and dance, Miss Oh?" Chong Won asks her. "What can *we* do?"

Miss Oh considers and answers simply, as one who will be helping them in the field of music appreciation. "One thing is that you two can try writing and composing music! Why not?"

The boys react with surprise and delight. They look at one another with wonder, and hold the gaze. Then, they begin to giggle with youthful excitement, as if an invisible hand is tickling them. This time, Chong Won answers, "O.K. Miss Oh, we will help the development of Common-labor Farmers music. Yes, we will." He smiles widely, and turns to his brother. Then, they simultaneously nod agreement to each other.

Then, Miss Oh stands and leaves to join the band where the village is gathered, and, as everyone is finished eating, they all watch together. The celebration continues with Farmers music and dance. Suddenly, Hong Won jumps up, excuses himself and carries their dishes to the cleaning area.

Young Kim sings the lead part, as he jumps and spins his body in acrobatic circles. The band marches and dances in a line behind him. Soon, all the people are on their feet, cheering and waving their arms as they attentively watch the band.

Now, everybody happily sings the traditional farmers songs with the band. The hoe washing celebration is successful because everyone is included, and everyone participates. The fields have produced a good crop this season, and they all feel enthusiastic to gratefully and joyfully celebrate the triumph.

But, not all the harvesting has been done. It will be done in the weeks about the time of the *Eighth Moon of the lunar calendar*[5], which is the moon of the fifteenth of August.

That is the day which Miss Oh has been anticipating almost every day, for it is the day of her future mother-

---

5. *Chusok*

in-law's wedding anniversary. More meaningful to her, however, is that it is the annual day that the women of their village—and the entire nation—are able to commemorate the patriotic event, of centuries before. That is the day of the beautiful, hillside dance, *Kanggangsullae*.

Young Kim also thinks about stimulating memories of the Eighth Moon. He likes the Autumn Night for the same reason that most men like it. Everyone has their chance to wrestle in a big, village competition. This native Korean wrestling[6] is Korea's established style, and so men highly value the competitive fun, which brings public recognition of able-bodied athletes with it.

However, this year, Young Kim's heart is set on something more important than wrestling. Why? Because, he knows that on the hoe cleaning day and the 'wet chori' day, his engagement to Miss Oh is planned to be announced! Now, he is at a point where the plans for the wedding are being finalized, and this traditional festival day, 'Autumn Night', is the day when the village will assemble again. Young Kim is very excited, because that day is when they hope to announce their wedding date!

This day is also a big day for the farmers who know that the fruit and grain harvest is near. From the day of washing of hoes, each farmer tends his own plot, while the produce of the commonly-owned land ripens. The days pass so rapidly, much to the delight of Miss Oh and Young Kim—and *Chusok* has finally arrived!

"Put on the clean clothes Miss Oh brought for you, Chong Won, and Hong Won," Ki Jun tells the boys. "Then you can run up the hill with the other children, and play sports with them."

---

6. *Ssirum*

"Yippee," the boys loudly shout together. "*Chusok* is here! Yippee." The boys love this Autumn Moon celebration, just as everybody does. The farmers know that this harvest will exceed that of the previous year. They enjoy increased satisfaction since they know that there is an increased need from the addition of the new families from the next village; and they must be totally dependent upon this harvest time.

Kyung Jae oversees the harvest of some fruit trees to help assure that the correct, limited quantity is picked. The interim labor force is here to supplement what has been picked in the last few days. They are harvesting persimmons, pears and pine nuts. This produce will be used to prepare the Autumn Night feast. The women have been working hard to prepare a good meal for this great day—for all the community.

Most of the village children have already gone up the hill to play sports together. Each child is dressed in clean clothes, especially for this day, and appears clean and bright, much like in a story book. Mothers laugh to think of this day each year. They all know that no matter how hard the children try to stay out of the dirt and mud— even *if* they try—that when evening arrives, their once clean clothes will be thoroughly embedded with layers of dirt and dried mud.

More *special* joys of Autumn Night! Even in the joint-labor village, there are traditional competitions on this day. For the women, it is a weaving competition. In fact, Dan Bae won the first place prize last year for weaving two sets of children's sports clothes. She had a need for them, last year—but now, although not anticipated, she will be able to give play clothes to the young boys who are newly adopted. She is happy that she has at least something to give them for this big day. Thus, many of the village women are busy in the weaving competition. They are working on a variety of forms. Some are weaving floor carpets; some weave shawls; and some curtains. They all use traditional patterns for their work. This weaving time is a favorite time for the women. They can accomplish much in one day, such as taking the opportunity to share creative ideas with one another while they create the long-planned weaving patterns, all the while enjoying one-another's company.

For the men, wrestling is as popular as the archery competition. Archery is not practiced as much, but there are still those who can amaze most villagers with their accuracy. Like *Tae Kwan Do*, wrestling is something that the men can do in casual moments throughout the year to keep alert and to keep their bodies in tone and more limber.

Although he has not participated in years, Kyung Jae still has a keen interest in Korean wrestling. He watches as a farmers music band member wrestles another young man, in one of the wrestling areas prepared especially for this Autumn Night event. Kyung Jae cheers heartily as the competition heightens. "His" Farmers band man is doing well in the match!

"Hello. I have the answer to your question, Mr. Farmers band leader," says Jae Kyung, who seems to appear from nowhere, unexpectedly. Kyung Jae is surprised to hear this man and see him appear at his side, especially so unexpectedly.

Kyung Jae is *very* surprised. The surprise is expressed in his eyes and face. The visitor bows slightly as he steps to face Kyung Jae. "Hello," Kyung Jae responds with a polite bow. "It is a surprise to see you here, now. But it is the best day of the year for our community to celebrate the blessings of unity. Everybody is enjoying this time!" "It is good that you can be easily fulfilled, Farmers band leader," answers Jae Kyung. "My needs in life are not as easily fulfilled as yours and those of your community. And surely, they are fulfilled in a much different way."

"I am sorry that you do not find enjoyment in a simple celebration. Today may be a day of change for you; and you may have a joyful day, just as we will. We have always enjoyed this day, with open hearts," responds Kyung Jae with simplicity that sounds innocent.

"Mr. Leader, you asked me a question when we last talked together," the visitor says. He thinks that his host will not be prepared for what he is about to say. He thinks that this saying may silence the man who differs with values that so many accept as productive. "Now I am able to tell you the answer," the visitor, Jae Kyung, says. "The answer is simple," says the man from the troupe of strolling actors. "Just eat, drink, and be merry!" he says, and laughs. His laugh betrays the deeply creased eyes from much worldly living. "Why must there be anything to make life any more complicated? We already have Confucius, who lived long ago and left his deep thoughts for the ages. We do not need to repeat thinking the deep thoughts that great men have thought before us. It is like I said; just let us eat, drink and be merry. Life will take care of itself, *Ture leader*[7]. It will take of itself."

"I hope that you can learn more of how life takes care of itself while you are here, today," Kyung Jae says. His hope is mixed with some disappointment. "Here, in the

---

7. *Yonggwa*

volunteer-labor community, we live by a pervasive norm. Everybody has the same minimum standards, which are expected of him or her. Thus, nobody is given absolute favor over another in social matters. And, nobody is considered lower than any other."

"We acknowledge excellence in leadership and in contributing to the village's well-being," Kyung Jae explains to his guest. "But there are not any who 'rule' over any other. I hope from this day, you too, will be helped to increase your ability to enjoy your life," concludes Kyung Jae, who bows deeply with respect for his visitor. He is touched within, almost hoping against hope for his guest.

"Thank you, Mr. Leader, Jae Kyung answers, without emotion. May you enjoy life as much as I. Goodbye!"

Kyung Jae forces himself not to dwell upon this dark cloud which is blowing through his life. He sees that this dark cloud is heavy, and the wind pushing it through is a strong wind. He has determined that it is a cloud which would run its course, no matter what else happens—still, Kyung Jae speaks silently to the One who places the clouds in the sky, for the sake of this fellow countryman. So, his thoughts turn back to the attractions of the day's activities.

The gongs resound, giving the signal for the announcement of the prize for the 'all-village wrestling competition'. Kyung Jae is drawn into the flow of people moving in one direction toward the main wrestling area. The prizes will be given in this area following the matches. Then, he sees the two new, young community members, Chong Won and Hong Won.

As apprentice herds-boys, they are participating in yet another privilege of their new vocations. They are given the opportunity to lead *the grand prize* into the wrestling area. The two boys are excited as they lead the 'Autumn Night Cow' into the circle. This cow, which has been given special care and very well fattened especially for this day is so much fatter than the other cows. It is to be awarded to the wrestling competition winner and his family.

This prize means as much to the village men of this community as to men in other traditional wrestling competitions. Why? It is because the people of this village do not practice the popular tradition of offering food at the graves of ancestors, or to village idols. Instead, the village compensates one family with a very substantial gift, for the excellence of one competitor in athletics. Therefore, the boys now guide the 'Autumn Night cow' into the midst of the people. The boys both grin with excitement. Soon, their faces become sober with humble awe, as they realize the dignity of their opportunity and task. Still, neither boy is able to stop grinning for very long!

The dead are remembered, while the living are joyously honored. The man chosen to administrate the competition now steps up on the tree stump to begin the announcements of the prizewinner. The village's band begins a flourish with gongs and drums to draw attention to the honored ones and to enthusiastically encourage the people to full enjoyment.

"Now, *ladies and gentlemen*[8], we have an excellent reward for the man who has maintained the best health of his body and has learned to develop his skill in protecting it and exercising it with our own Korean style

8. *Yorobun*

wrestling," the organizer announces. "This reward is one which has been produced here in our midst, all year long. It is the fatted 'Autumn Night cow'." The people cheer and applaud in response to the announcement off the generous reward.

"It is with pleasure and honor that we present the prize to our own 'discipliner of the idle', Samuel Lee." Again, the people cheer loudly and surge up toward the awards area. "Our number-one, award-winning wrestler has also disciplined seven opponents today, and we honor that with the reward of the cow which we have made ready for months. May you and your family long enjoy and remember this prize!"

"Thank you *assisting officer* [9]," replies Mr. Lee, humbly. "The honor goes to the Giver of health, discipline, and the divine principles by which we live—and are being blessed. The honor goes to the God of heaven!" he proclaims. The crowd roars its approval.

As Mr. Lee concludes, he bows from atop the stump, and with humility keeps lowering his head until he just steps down and touches the ground. With a smile covering is face, he takes the rope from Chong Won and begins to admire the new supply of future meals for him and his entire family.

As the band plays and dances in his honor, he leaps for joy with them. Quickly, Kyung Jae jumps onto the stump and the band soon becomes silent. Now, he announces, "We cannot let this most beautiful day pass without remembering to thank the women patriots, who dance as a memorial to the battle strategy of the woman's patriotic dance. This day is one always to be remem-

---

9. *Togam*

bered. For me, and for my family, it is all the more not to be forgotten, for it also is the anniversary day of meeting my wife. Now, I would like to make a surprise announcement," Kyung Jae says to the crowd which has grown silent and ready to listen. "My son has asked me to let this day be as special to him as it has been to my wife and me.

Today, we are celebrating Autumn Night. To me, it is the most beautiful night of the year.

"This is truly a day of thanksgiving! Can there be a more romantic day to express a commitment of love— for an entire lifetime?" Kyung Jae says, as a challenge to the entire crowd.

"No, no, no!" the crowd shouts, chanting a unified response. "At this time, I would like to invite someone to come forward; the person who is skilled in discovering if two people will be truly compatible. Mrs. Chun is our marriage mediator. Mrs. Chun, we all welcome you."

With this, Kyung Jae bows and lifts his hand. The crowd cheers for him, and for Mrs. Chun's sake—as much as for the newly engaged couple.

Mrs. Chun begins to speak to the crowd. She bows and says, "I came to your village to investigate this couple, to learn if they would be compatible and be 'right' for each other. I came with the pretense that I wanted to investigate Farmers music and dance. Did anybody believe me? Maybe not! Even so, I must apologize and ask forgiveness for not being honest in your village. Especially, since I am a stranger here. It isn't always easy for many people to trust a stranger."

"Moreover, a *love marriage* that also uses a mediator is rare. So, I am honored to be here with you. Thank you for your invitation," Mrs. Chun says. She really feels as

if she successfully completed her assigned task; and very
effectively!

CHAPTER XVIII

AS YOU DO TO THE LEAST OF THESE

Tradition demands a balanced beginning on the day before the wedding—that is, tradition, combined with innovation! Superstitious practices are replaced with the performance of more 'contemporary' rites, according to the time-tested social and faith standards of the common-labor community. Young Kim rides on horseback to the house of Miss Oh, accompanied by his cousin. His cousin carries the lacquered box, closely keeping to tradition. The box contains the skirt and blouse or coat for the marriage ceremony. Later that evening, Young Kim's cousin presents Miss Oh's father with the lacquered box at his house. Miss Oh's father is careful to keep with tradition when he makes sure that his little son rubs charcoal on Young Kim's cousin's face when he delivers the 'lacquered box' to the bride's father. The family laughs at this tradition, a lighthearted break from the tensions of the time of the marriage. *The time* truly has arrived!

At the moment that the couple of honor is prepared to come to the place at which Mrs. Chun had spoken, Young Kim slowly approaches and stands at her side. Miss Oh is hidden from view on the far side. She is behind a tent-like enclosure constructed between the pines, made especially for her preparation. The couple each is to remain silent as the introductions proceed.

At the correct time, the soon-to-be groom steps slowly to the center of the pine-ringed clearing and bows with all possible respect and ceremony. He bows by lowering himself to his knees, and bows until his head touches his hands, which are braced before him on the ground. Here, there must be no compromise.

Then, he gracefully arises. After this first bow, he is given a live goose with its feet and beak tied with red silk. Young Kim's father favors this ancient custom because it is another practice that gives honor to the Creator, through symbolism. Through His natural creation, a reflection of manifested faithfulness of the Creator can be seen. The bird is believed to be a symbol of fidelity to the ancestors of the modern inheritors of this sacred ceremony.

For, if a goose in the wild dies, its spouse will never mate again. This is one traditional value, which Kyung

Jae and Dan Bae desire to pass on to the next generation and to publicly proclaim it—just as generations of
Koreans have done before them. Unexplainably, Young
Kim feels wonderfully closer to his Creator, as he bows,
with this creature of marvelous beauty clutched firmly
under his arm. With the feel of the red earth on his hands, and the
scent of the pines in his head, Young Kim kneels and
is filled with adoration for this precious, rare, lifetime
event. This event is unique for he and his lifelong partner-
to-be, due to the wonderful beauty of all that surrounds
him, as well. As his head touches the back of his hand, he
breathes a deep breath of thanks to heaven. With joyful
excitement, his heart beats harder and his temples lightly
throb as the blood surges to his bowed and lowered head.

The people turn their heads as the curtain opens and
two middle-aged women guide the bride toward the
center area. There, Young Kim arises in strength and dignity. Miss Oh is dressed in *the traditional blouse, and* full
skirt [1]. She is dressed in rose color above, and bright pink
below. Dan Bae and Kyung Jae carefully chose and con-
sulted with the prospective bride and groom regarding
every detail of the marriage ceremony. All those invited
prefer a good balance of traditional elements, while
omitting the superfluous, suppressive, or even ungodly.

The bride is now escorted forth, not withholding her
smile — although this is contrary to what tradition would
have predestined. Such a breach with canon tradition
would have dictated only female offspring, according to
traditional thought! A serious gaze, consistent with the

---

1. *chogori*, blouse, and *chima*, skirt. The *'hanbok'*, the two-piece,
traditional dress.

penetrating and enduring spirit of the marriage rite, tempers her lovely and shining expression from time to time.

Still, her simple, clear beauty is enhanced as the bright red blush is applied to her cheeks. However, the traditional, accompanying splash of dominant red forehead blaze is absent. She wears a small rose-colored, crown-like cushion in her hair with several glistening beaded stickpins securing it to her smoothly combed jet-black hair, fastened just above her neck. Young Kim's bride's radiant beauty is all the millennia-old tradition could possibly have offered

Then, Miss Oh gracefully steps up to and across the mat spread in font of and in the center of the area, and begins to make a deep, slow and graceful bow. Her arms are still being guided by the two matrons who hold her hands as she curtsies very low—almost to a sitting position. With equal grace and solemnity, she slowly rises to an upright position, still full of composure. She repeats the inspiring curtsy two more times, according to the dictates of proper tradition, and the groom approaches the far end of the mat to make his bows.

The fragrance of pine scent refreshes every wedding guest, a timely gift for the occasion, and the people are happy. Still, not everyone agrees that some traditions are to be constantly practiced, despite the unity of mind of most of the community. In contrast, others feel just as strongly that more traditions should remain. Those present reason to that end, because they believe that all traditions contribute to the continuation of a 'more Korean' life.

Unity is not uncommon, however. Nobody can remember except for a few times that even a simple dispute arose about tradition in day-to-day living. The value of a *giving and forgiving community* is too great for individuals to act out of character by expressing isolated ideas, or extreme personal biases.

Everyone present is both content and excited about every detail of the ceremony, and like the appreciative silence at a symphonic performance, golden silence is kept, and no critical word is spoken, nor even thought. Thus, a festive spirit remains fresh and pure and that spirit electrifies the air.

A table is placed—with both common, staple food and beautifully arranged rare delicacies—behind the ceremonial mat, upon which the couple sits, on either side. Priorities are kept in order as Young Kim responds to his partner's bows. His own deep and sincere bows are made in response to those, which have touched and penetrated his heart. Young Kim silently thanks the God of Heaven that his eyes do not show the mist that he feels— from the awesome beauty of his fiancé and the décor and the grace of the ceremony presented before him.

How inspiring it all is! He bows deeply twice, then again only half way down. Again, tradition is broken when the pair is seated.

The glass of liquor is brought by the bridesmaids to be sipped by the groom. After Miss Oh's lace-veiled hands touch the glass, the wine is then sipped by Young Kim and returned to Miss Oh. She joins Young Kim in sharing life by sharing the cup—the symbol of life—by which millions have been brought into a purified state of the mystical union of holy marriage.

According to custom, the process of sipping is repeated three times. Smiles make everlasting impressions on the couple's hearts, as Miss Oh, herself is impressed more with the expectation of hope in Divine promise. Those promises bring forth her own realization; precious, and of inestimable value, rather than within the bounds of traditional ritual.

Miss Oh has more than just a smile or her lips, and more than the smile which joy has produced. The expression on her face is of that part of her heart which reveals itself to the watching eyes of each individual who would ask, "Is she able to overcome obstacles that her predecessors before her have overcome?" Intense joy is shared between the two and as Young Kim lifts his eyes, he can clearly see that the joy *is* being shared. And, it is as an interconnecting band—which unites all present at the ceremony.

The symbol of communal sustenance is shared, and the ladies return again to the middle of the mat, between the seated couple, with the goose. Again, here is a creature, itself the symbol of the bond of the lifelong commitment they will both make. Now, the red thread is removed from the bird's beak.

This time the couple's go-between feeds the goose from her hand with vermicelli noodles, as has also been traditionally done, for generations.

The women elders now go to join the guests, and Young Kim walks to the bridal chamber to change. Quickly, he emerges in a white robe. He looks very handsome, and Miss Oh feels like she is dreaming of heaven.

Miss Oh enters the chamber and sits upon a big, soft cushion, still in a dreamlike state. There, she first receives, and bows to guests from outside the village. The couple is now married!

This couple-of-honor has broken with ancient tradition because they became friends before their engagement and wedding. This is not an uncommon occurrence now, in modern times. Still, for centuries, if the engaged couple would see each other before the day before the wedding, it was an unacceptable and marriage-preventing practice, as Young Kim and Miss Oh have now done. Nevertheless, now young people are being married in 'love marriages'. The 'love marriage' is the kind that Kyung Jae always wanted to experience, for he is old enough to have seen the practice of common relationship of minimal contact and minimal communication.

Like his father, Young Kim understands the difference between a contract and the marriage covenant. Young Kim also knows, since it has recently been brought to his attention, that it is the Father's will to expand the Ture Nongak band's horizons for the Gospel's sake —even to the ends of the world! His wife will be there at his side, wherever he goes. For marriage was designed to be a three-person partnership, from the beginning of the world.

Kyung Jae also knows that this is a time of great and positive change in the land. For, he and Dan Bae both see and know that love without reservation or compromise is what so many on the peninsula yearn for. They know that for centuries and centuries, love which has been missing for so long, is realized in the established presence of their God—who is incontestably, the God of their ancestors, the God of Heaven, *'Hananim'*, the Great One!

THE END/KYOMAL

GLOSSARY

Aboji, Father.

Annyong haseyo, the common Korean greeting-an equivalent of 'Shalom', or 'total well-being to you'. It may be used at all times of day.

cha, tea.

chigae, a traditional Korean staple serving of soup-stew consistency.

ching, a large gong; one of several percussion instruments in a farmers band.

Chipsa—the title of honor for leaders and organizers of groups.

Chosun, the ancient name of Korea, meaning (Land of) *The Morning Calm.*

Chusok, one of two annual Korean 'thanksgivings', celebrated on the 8th lunar full-moon month. It is popularly called, 'Autumn night'.

han, is the Korean term for 'incurable suffering' of the soul; the enduring suffering of the 'Korean, national heart'.

Hananim, the primitive and contemporary Korean name of the Highest Deity/God of Heaven. Translated, 'The Great One', also understood as 'The God of

Heaven' and 'The Greatest One; the number One Sir/Lord'. The One, 'Supreme God' of ancient, pre-Buddhist, pre-Taoist and pre-Confucian, Korean and Chinese history.

heung, 'style'. One of two essential elements in the farmers band; the other being *meut*, enthusiasm.

homi ssish, lit. 'washing of hoes'. The community celebration at the end of the farm season.

Hwarang. A select, multi-talented group, assembled centuries ago, as 'Knights of Korea'. Originally Buddhist-elite, multi-talented, respected poets, writers and singers, they were also trained to fight to defend the 'honor of the land'. Their ranks evolved in the entertainment world, and they thus moved away from their ideal, original stages.

juche, is the 'salvation motto' of the regime of the North, meaning 'self-reliance'.

kalbi, pork ribs. A main, meat staple in the Korean diet.

kibun, the important communication of one's state of being through the eyes. Thus, the eyes are the keys to the being, disclosing a 'right mood' or any other, less desirable state. One responds sensitively to one's *kibun*—the premier rule is not to disturb one's kibun!

kim chee, or kimchee, a very popular & famous Korean staple of spicy, marinated cabbage, radish or greens, traditionally made in large batches and stored for the winter in the ground in large clay vessels for natural refrigeration.

kut, ritual or rite, used here, in conjunction with either shaman or folk-religion band rituals. The word is often modified by the specific kind of rite, such as *nongak kut*—farmers band rite, and *mudang kut*—folk religionist rite.

kwaenggwari, the small gong. Instrument used by the band leader, who uses the resounding tone of the gong to lead the others. It is held in one hand and played with a small stick with the other.

meut, (pronounced 'mutt'). Enthusiasm, which is said to be an essential in the performance of good Farmers music and dance..

Minjung, term for the common people, or the oppressed masses.

Mudang, folk-religionist. The most numerous (approx. 700,000, plus) in present-day Korea is usually a female, 'evil-breaking' worker who uses musical instruments to accompany her in-home rituals.

Namsadang p'ae, Korean words for a 'group of professional musicians', a.k.a. 'group of Strolling Actors' and '*Specialized* Farmers Music and Dance'.

nongak, nong is farm/farmers, *ak* (or ahk) is music (and dance, in this context.); thus, Farmers music and dance. The use of this word also implies, in this context, the (word) *band*, as well.

nonggi, a large, Korean banner; now also a popular advertising tool, in urban areas.

nong chong, Nong is farm and *chong* is office, or storage shed.

ondol, sub-floor heating system; one of Korea's many ancient innovative inventions.

pos'u, traditional hunter's folk drama.

pulgogi, (bulgogi) beef. A popular staple, traditionally was/is usually cooked at the table using a perforated pan or grill.

Sangsoe, a band leader.

Shang Di, the Chinese name for God that corresponds with the Korean, *Hananim,* that was/is used in both primitive and contemporary China.

Solsori, lead singer of the farmers band.

Ssirum, Korean wrestling.

Togam, assisting officer.

tongil, reunification. The word for the hope for reconciliation, used by millions in separated families, and in the political arena.

Tonggori, relatives.

Ture/Doorae, (two spellings are given due to the pronunciation, according to the popular, contemporary, Hangul system of spelling and pronunciation.) It is the *'co-operative, common, volunteer, or mutual-*labor (synonymous, interchangeable terms) associations of Korean, rural history.

Ture/Doorae Nongak, Volunteer-labor Farmers Music and Dance (band). A combination of *Ture/Doorae,* and *Nongak* (see both words, above). *Farmers* is primarily plural, as used herein, suitable for the title, and possession can be inferred.

'Wet chori', the name given to a feast of the co-operative labor community.

Yangban, a term originally reserved for the intellectual elite, instituted in the Confucian era—historically, a group of career, government officials who obtained their posts by excelling on a government exam.

yobo, term of endearment reserved for married couples.

Yongjwa/Yonggwa, a leader of a community, or community group—Ture/Doorae leader.

Yorobun, Ladies and gentlemen.

'TURE NONGAK'
Common-labor Farmers Music and Dance
An historical novel

ORDERING INFORMATON

Mail orders to:
> Billy Lee
> 7085 Battle Creek Rd. SE
> Salem, OR 97317

Please provide the following information:
> Name, address, city, zip,
> Quantity of copies desired @ $_____
> Shipping & handling $1.75 first copy
> $1.00 for each additional copy

CPSIA information can be obtained at www.ICGtesting.com
Printed in the USA
BVOW032116020812

296951BV00001B/21/P